IDENTITY

reset

FIONA PYSZKA

ISBN-13: 978-0-9883461-7-8

For further information please contact
Fiona Pyszka by visiting www.fionainc.com
or write to the office of Fiona Inc.

P O Box 154
Hummelstown, PA 17036

ISBN-13: 978-0-9883461-7-8

Scripture references from the Kings James Version of the Bible, unless otherwise noted.

DEDICATION

To my Lord and Savior for creating me for such a time as this. I am privileged to work in Your Kingdom

To my husband and children. Your continuous support of the purpose and plans that God has for my life is amazing.

To all of you. God has created you with a special plan and purpose that you have the honor of fulfilling. I applaud you today to go forth and accomplish all that our Great God has blessed you to do.

Table of Contents

ACKNOWLEDGMENTS

Thank you to my husband, Doug, for his help in making the content of this book understandable for you.

Thank you to Lisa Schmidt and Abigail Hall for your endless hours of editing expertise. You are amazing and this book would not have been what it is today without your help. Thank you!

INTRODUCTION

You have been created with an identity that no other person has -- one that is as unique as your fingerprint. God *designed* you to do something that no one else can do. The tragedy is that many people believe lies about themselves and despise the very design that God gave them. They live life trying to be someone they are not, and end up fighting the wrong battle -- trying to change themselves when all along God has designed them to change the world.

In this book, you will learn to embrace the *you* that God created and walk in your destiny.

You will be able to recognize ways that the enemy has tried to mar your identity, and stop him in his tracks. If you have been struggling with issues like depression, identity crisis, or damaged self-esteem, it's time to be free.

Don't waste another minute living a mediocre life. Anything that has been disordered in you can easily be restored by your Creator. It's time for your identity reset.

FIONA PYSZKA

CHAPTER 1

God Made You

God's plan for you is so big that if you saw the whole thing now, you would probably start thinking of ways that you don't deserve to do what God has planned for you to do. Just take a look at our universe. Is any part of it mediocre? Does it lack any support? Can it sustain itself? Think of the stars in the sky and how awesome it is to see the beauty of God's creation.

All of these systems work effortlessly day and night. They are given seasons and cycles to keep at optimum performance at the Creator's command. The sun has not dimmed since its creation. The moon has not missed a cycle since it was designed. The oceans have not passed their boundaries since God put them in their place and told them to stay there. All of these created systems and galaxies by God have kept their identity since their creation. Why? Because God created them and they obeyed God's command to them. God shares this with Job, as He explains to Job His greatness.

Job 38:8-11 (AMP) - 8 "Or who enclosed the sea with doors. When it burst forth and went out of the womb;9 When I made the clouds its garment. And thick darkness its swaddling band,10 And marked for it My [appointed] boundary. And set bars and doors [defining the shorelines],11 And said, 'This far you shall come, but no farther; And here your proud waves shall stop'?

Your identity is more important to God than the elaborate systems He created to keep the universe in existence. God physically created each person the same way. He took two cells from two different sources, male and female, and He formed you. Yet, each person has a unique identity. He designed you intricately in your mother's womb. It is there that He put your unique design. No one else has your fingerprint; no one has your ear shape; no one has your DNA.

Psalm 139:13-15 (NLT) - 13 You made all the delicate, inner parts of my body and knit me together in my mother's womb.14 Thank you for making me so wonderfully complex! Your workmanship is marvelous—how well I know it.15 You watched me as I was being formed in utter seclusion, as I was woven together in the dark of the womb.

God secretly formed every part of you. His design of you is so secret that no one can replicate you. The closest man has come to replicating a human is a robot version doing some of the functions of a human, but never all. No matter the advancement of science, creation of man is God's design, and He holds the patent.

You are a patented design of God. No one else will ever be created who carries your unique identity. This is how important and priceless you are to God. You are the only one like you. Even the sun or the moon can't make such a claim, as there are suns and moons on other planets. The oceans can't make those claims either. Only humans can make that claim. You can!

Psalm 139:16 (NLT) - 16 You saw me before I was born. Every day of my life was recorded in your book. Every moment was laid out before a single day had passed.

The reason you're here at all is because God made you, saw you and approved of you. <u>God has approved of you!</u> We see the model of God's creation and approval process in Genesis. Before He considered His creation complete, He put a stamp of approval on it and His stamp of approval says "good".

Genesis 1:3-4 (NLT) - 3 Then God said, "Let there be light," and there was light. 4 And God saw that the light was good. Then he separated the light from the darkness.

God did not separate the light from the darkness until He saw that the light was good. He would not put light that was just "okay" on the earth; the light that He wanted to have here had to be good. There had to be a distinction between the light and the darkness, enough to separate the two. How about you? Your distinction is good enough to separate you from the rest of your family and peers. God knows your difference and He approves of it and thinks it's good.

How do we know God approved of you? Maybe you're thinking that your arrival here was not exactly the "sanctioned" way of coming. Maybe you were told that you were a mistake, your parents had you out of wedlock, or you may have been born as a result of rape or incest. These circumstances are less than ideal, but you as a human being, a person, are not less than ideal. You are not what man labels you; you are what God created. He wrote all about you before He brought you live and in person to the earth.

There was a man named Jeremiah with insecurities, just as you may have. You may have questions about being capable of being "good" enough to be here or to be utilized for God's work.

Jeremiah 1:4-10 (KJV) - 4 Then the word of the Lord came unto me, saying,

5 Before I formed thee in the belly I knew thee; and before thou camest forth out of the womb I sanctified thee, and I ordained thee a prophet unto the nations.

6 Then said I, Ah, Lord God! behold, I cannot speak: for I am a child.

7 But the Lord said unto me, Say not, I am a child: for thou shalt go to all that I shall send thee, and whatsoever I command thee thou shalt speak.

8 Be not afraid of their faces: for I am with thee to deliver thee, saith the Lord.

9 Then the Lord put forth his hand, and touched my mouth. And the Lord said unto me, Behold, I have put my words in thy mouth.

10 See, I have this day set thee over the nations and over the kingdoms, to root out, and to pull down, and to destroy, and to throw down, to build, and to plant.

In one conversation with God, Jeremiah's insecurities received God's attention and answers were given as to who Jeremiah was created to be and what he was created to do.

Excuses about your capabilities when God asks for your

help will never hold up against the amazing design by which you were created. God can answer any questions about your ability you dare to ask.

Your mind is capable of being renewed daily. You body is capable of being healed. Mountains can be moved at your words. You have the ability to receive power to cause the dead to come back to life. How amazing you are. You're God's creation. You're God's human. A person created in God's image. How amazing you are indeed!

Romans 12:2 (KJV) - 2 And be not conformed to this world: but be ye transformed by the renewing of your mind, that ye may prove what is that good, and acceptable, and perfect, will of God.

Jeremiah 17:14 (KJV) - 14 Heal me, O Lord, and I shall be healed; save me, and I shall be saved: for thou art my praise.

Mark 11:23 (KJV) - 23 For verily I say unto you, That whosoever shall say unto this mountain, Be thou removed, and be thou cast into the sea; and shall not doubt in his heart, but shall believe that those things which he saith shall come to pass; he shall have whatsoever he saith.

Matthew 10:8 (KJV) - 8 Heal the sick, cleanse the lepers, raise the dead, cast out devils: freely ye have received, freely give.

All of these verses prove the ability of God in you to do exploits beyond the capabilities of planets, stars, the sun or moon. They cannot do what you can do. The sun cannot speak to a mountain to be removed; the sun cannot raise the dead or bring healing to the sick. But you can! You are the only creation that can be empowered by God to do what Jesus did and what God can do. Except for angels, no other creation has the privilege to operate in God's power.

Luke 9:1 (AMP) - 9 Now Jesus called together the twelve [disciples] and gave them [the right to exercise] power and authority over all the demons and to heal diseases.

You have been given power and authority over your enemy. God has empowered you. No other creation on earth has this empowerment. Instead, they are subject to your dominion.

Genesis 1:26 (AMP) - 26 Then God said, "Let Us (Father, Son, Holy Spirit) make man in Our image, according to Our likeness [not physical, but a spiritual personality and moral likeness]; and let them have complete authority over the fish of the sea, the birds of the air, the cattle, and over the entire earth, and over everything that creeps and crawls on the earth."

You even have authority over the sun! We see this authority demonstrated in the story of Joshua in battle. He was fighting and had not yet won, and the sun was setting. Joshua needed the sun to stand still until he was finished with his fight, so he told it to stand still.

Joshua 10:12-13 (AMP) - 12 Then Joshua spoke to the Lord on the day when the Lord handed over the Amorites to the sons of Israel, and Joshua said in the sight of Israel, "Sun, stand still at Gibeon, And moon, in the Valley of Aijalon."

13 So the sun stood still, and the moon stopped,

Until the nation [of Israel] took vengeance upon their enemies.

Is it not written in the Book of Jashar? So the sun stood still in the middle of the sky and was in no hurry to go down for about a whole day.

Joshua was not created in a special lab with superpowers added to him. He was created by God, just like you. He was designed to help God in His exploits against the enemy. Joshua used his God-given power and abilities to fight the enemy he was pursuing. He was able to cause the sun to stand still and the moon to stop. Joshua stopped cycles that were in place to cause the earth to function. He stopped it with his mouth.

Do you see yourself taking authority over the elements like Joshua did? Maybe you think these things could only happen once in a lifetime. The truth is, Joshua was a son, he was a follower of Moses, and he was a leader. He was stuck in the wilderness with all the complainers even though he was not in agreement with their complaint. Joshua was an everyday guy who did everyday things to live. Yet, he used his mouth to stop the sun. What can you do with your mouth to change your world?

God's design of you was not just so you can survive hard times or tell nice stories to people. His design of you was to carry His power and authority on the earth, to dominate and take over where the enemy is still camping. His design for you is to be exactly who He created you to be before the foundations of the world.

Ephesians 1:4 (AMP) - 4 just as [in His love] He chose us in Christ [actually selected us for Himself as His own] before the foundation of the world, so that we would be holy [that is, consecrated, set apart for Him, purpose-driven] and blameless in His sight.

You are here for such a time as this to do a work that no one else imagine is possible for you to do. Your unique identity gives you access to places that no one else could access. You can defy nature and live. You can do the impossible and live to tell about it. Your story could change the world. Remember the story of Daniel in the lions' den, or David and Goliath, or Joseph as Prime Minister? These people all defied the odds of what was possible, yet they overcame and did it anyway. Their unique identity allowed them the favor and power to do what they did.

How can we access our unique identity to do exploits for God? It's easier than you think, and available for those who want to participate. Let's take a look.

CHAPTER 2

Identity For Your Destiny

You were designed after the likeness and in the image of God. This design puts you at a complete advantage over any other created being or thing in the world. Even angels cannot make such a profession.

Genesis 1:26 (AMP) - 26 Then God said, "Let Us (Father, Son, Holy Spirit) make man in Our image, according to Our likeness [not physical, but a spiritual personality and moral likeness]; and let them have complete authority over the fish of the sea, the birds of the air, the cattle, and over the entire earth, and over everything that creeps and crawls on the earth."

You were not only created with dominion mandates, but with identity markers that set you apart from other people. God sees each person as an individual, knowing exactly what assignments He's put in them to fulfill. God is not into doing cookie-cutter creation. Look at the diversity in flowers, trees and animals. God designs signature goods.

There is a reason for each person being uniquely identified in the earth: it causes us to be recognized by our assignment. Just as homes and governments have unique identifiers for their residents, God has unique identifiers for us to operate as agents of His Kingdom on earth.

Imagine living in a home where there were septuplets, and

all seven of them had the same name, whether male or female. Could you fathom the chaos of getting the attention of just one. Every time you needed to call one of them, they would all come running, because you're speaking an identifier, their name, that they all have in common. There would be mass confusion which would incite high levels of frustration. Instead it is common practice to have unique names for each member of the household. Each person may carry the same last name, but their first name is unique to them.

This system of unique identification not only works in a home, but in a country as well. Each citizen or resident is given a unique identification number. These numbers hold data pertaining to that person's life. In other words, the numbers hold their identity records. Without the knowledge of their numbers, they cannot access their rights and privileges as citizens of the country. Proper identity is necessary to prove ownership and membership.

It's the same concept in God's design of you. Your unique identity known only to God and to the places and people He has assigned you to, gives you access to doors and opportunities that no one else can unlock.

Knock and The Door Will Be Opened

Have you ever been in a situation where someone assumed that you couldn't do something because they tried the same thing and it didn't work for them? Or maybe you have those feelings about yourself, as you look at a "successful" person in your life who has failed to do what God has asked you to do. You assume that if they can't make it, what makes you think you can make it? These thoughts are common in today's society, and many people fail because they buy into the misconception of this scenario. So what's the truth concerning this? You may be thinking it's only logical to assume that if many before you have tried and they've failed, why should you try? Here's why: If God asks you to do something, He knows that what He asks you to do will respond to your identity. The password needed to give you access to that door has been coded in your God-given identity.

Anything you do in life should be done under the leading and guiding of Holy Spirit. This is the marker that separates you from someone who is not a child of God. The scriptures clear this up for us.

Romans 8:14 (NLT) - 14 For all who are led by the Spirit of God are children of God.

You want to live as a child of God because a God-directed life includes protection from making wrong decisions. If you slip and do make wrong decisions, you also get help to restore you back to the place you should be. What a win-win situation to find yourself in, if you just decide to be led by Holy Spirit in your life.

Once you have made the decision and habitually live your life with the principle of being led by Holy Spirit, then the results others have had in what you're going to do have no bearing on your decision. You will no longer compare yourself to another person's results or lack thereof. You will instead get excited about what's behind the door, and you will just knock.

Luke 11:9-10 (NLT) - 9 "And so I tell you, keep on asking, and you will receive what you ask for. Keep on seeking, and you will find. Keep on knocking, and the door will be opened to you. 10 For everyone who asks, receives. Everyone who seeks, finds. And to everyone who knocks, the door will be opened.

Have you ever seen a biometric security system in operation? This is a system that requires a biological code to unlock the place of entrance. For example, you may have to scan your retina, or give a fingerprint or speak a phrase in order for the lock to unlock and the door to open. The lock opens only for specific people whose body characteristics have been pre-stored in the system. If the system recognizes the person, access is granted. If not, the person cannot enter.

God had the same concept in mind when He created you. He has prepared things for you to do in this life, on earth, today. In order for those places to be opened to you, you've got to show up and present yourself for a biometric scan of your identity.

You are to ask; speak by faith concerning what God has asked you to believe. *You are to seek*; look at the direction, keep focused, stare at the mark that God has given you as an assignment. *You are to keep on knocking;* let the DNA on your hands contact the door that is closed to you. In other words, put some work to the assignment. Don't wait until the door opens before you start the work: work (knock) so the door can be opened. It doesn't matter if someone else failed.

They failed because they did not have the correct biometrics. They did not have your identity markers set by God for the door to be opened.

Your identity matters to your assignment! There are some things on this earth that will only respond to your touch, your voice or your vision. No one else will do!

Moses

Moses was a man that was saved from death as a baby, to be the deliverer for the promise that God made to His people over 400 years earlier. At the time he was born there was a decree sent out by the king to kill all baby boys under the age of two years old.

Exodus 1:22 (KJV) - 22 And Pharaoh charged all his people, saying, Every son that is born ye shall cast into the river, and every daughter ye shall save alive.

Exodus 2:1-3 (KJV) - 2 And there went a man of the house of Levi, and took to wife a daughter of Levi.

2 And the woman conceived, and bare a son: and when she saw him that he was a goodly child, she hid him three months.

3 And when she could not longer hide him, she took for him an ark of bulrushes, and daubed it with slime and with pitch, and put the child therein; and she laid it in the flags by the river's brink.

Exodus 2:5-6 (KJV) - 5 And the daughter of Pharaoh came down to wash herself at the river; and her maidens walked along by the river's side; and when she saw the ark among the flags, she sent her maid to fetch it.

6 And when she had opened it, she saw the child: and, behold, the babe wept. And she had compassion on him, and said, This is one of the Hebrews' children.

Exodus 2:10 (KJV) - 10 And the child grew, and she brought him unto Pharaoh's daughter, and he became her son. And she called his name Moses: and she said, Because I drew him out of the water.

We see here the story of how a little boy was delivered from death. He was the only boy of his age recorded to have lived and not be thrown into the river. He may have been the only Hebrew male in his age category. So how did he end up living and not dying? His mama received wisdom from God to deliver him to the same hands that were trying to kill him. He became the son of Pharaoh's daughter, the king who decreed his death.

Because of his new living arrangement, he did not get to grow up in his own household. He did not have Hebrew friends; instead, his friends and peers were Egyptian boys. Moses lived in this foreign household until God was ready for his DNA to touch his God-given assignment. Moses was the chosen deliverer for the children of Israel from the hands of bondage. Moses was the leader who was preserved by God for the epic deliverance of the ages.

As Moses' story continues we see his rise to leadership in God's plan for the children of Israel. He was reluctant to do what God was asking of him, but God insisted. God needed Moses, because when God created the Red Sea it knew one day it would have to part to rescue God's people. The access code for this opening was embedded in Moses' identity. The Red Sea recognized it right away. Moses' voice code was custom coded to speak to Pharaoh and demand the release of God's people. Even though Aaron would do the speaking, the words had to first come from Moses' mouth. God had designed this a long time ago, and God knew what He designed to respond to Moses' voice before Moses was even born.

Exodus 4:15-16 (NLT) - 15 Talk to him, and put the words in his mouth. I will be with both of you as you speak, and I will instruct you both in what to do. 16 Aaron will be your spokesman to the people. He will be your mouthpiece, and you will stand in the place of God for him, telling him what to say.

What about you? Are you seeing a picture here of how God's plans are not haphazard? He doesn't just ask people to do things because there is no one else. He asks you, when His time is right, to do the things He preplanned for you to do. That is the time that people, places and atmospheres will respond to you. He preplanned doors to respond to your knock, people to listen to your voice, and places to give up what has been hidden for your seeking. Don't live life aimlessly. Understand that God has vision for your life.

Moses had the vision code to see the promised land. Before the people entered the land, Moses' eyes looked at it. I am convinced that Moses' look unlocked the land to be pursued by Joshua.

Numbers 27:12-14 (NLT) - 12 One day the Lord said to Moses, "Climb one of the mountains east of the river, and look out over the land I have given the people of Israel.

13 After you have seen it, you will die like your brother, Aaron,

14 for you both rebelled against my instructions in the wilderness of Zin. When the people of Israel rebelled, you failed to demonstrate my holiness to them at the waters." (These are the waters of Meribah at Kadesh in the wilderness of Zin.)

For years I wondered why God would take Moses to show him the land that he could never enter. I thought, "What a tease. What a cruel thing to have to experience." But in fact, Moses was a key component to the entrance of the land of promise.

Here's the principle: God set up an order for the earth which He himself honors. For God's plans to succeed on earth, He has put divine order in place. One such plan is the speaking of things on earth by someone before it can happen on earth. Therefore, to execute His plans, God has appointed prophets to speak what He wants to happen here. God's Kingdom is organized and well-managed by Him. He is not doing things in the spur of the moment, although sometimes it may seem so to you. He has a design and a plan. It all gets executed and works perfectly when we respond to His instructions. The prophet is a microphone for God's voice on earth. The prophet speaks and God does.

Amos 3:7 (NLT) - 7 Indeed, the Sovereign Lord never does anything until he reveals his plans to his servants the prophets.

Moses was taken to the mountain to see the promised land so he could finish the job God had prepared for him to do. God needed Moses to look at the promised land to unlock what God had promised the Israelites. Moses was the one designated to get the people to the land. He disqualified himself when he disobeyed God's instruction to have water provided for the people in the wilderness by speaking instead of striking (see Numbers 20:12-13). However, his job of seeing the promised land was still needed. Moses' retinal scan of the promised land was still necessary.

Here is the encounter between Moses and God when God called Moses to be the deliverer of God's people. Notice how Moses' original instruction was to take the people from Egypt to the promised land as described in verse 8 below.

Exodus 3:6-10 (NLT) - 6 I am the God of your father—the God of Abraham, the God of Isaac, and the God of Jacob." When Moses heard this, he covered his face because he was afraid to look at God.

7 Then the Lord told him, "I have certainly seen the oppression of my people in Egypt. I have heard their cries of distress because of their harsh slave drivers. Yes, I am aware of their suffering.

8 So I have come down to rescue them from the power of the Egyptians and lead them out of Egypt into their own fertile and spacious land. It is a land flowing with milk and honey—the land where the Canaanites, Hittites, Amorites, Perizzites, Hivites, and Jebusites now live.

9 Look! The cry of the people of Israel has reached me, and I have seen how harshly the Egyptians abuse them.

10 Now go, for I am sending you to Pharaoh. You must lead my people Israel out of Egypt."

God's Kingdom is a work of art and precision. He wanted to get His people to their rightful place. The people's delay to get into the promised land did not deter God from His plan. God waited until the right group was qualified to go in. Only the children of the generation that exited bondage were able to enter the true freedom God had prepared for His people. Why? Because the children of Israel did something with their voice that hindered the opening of the doors to the promised land. They believed an evil report about the land they were given and their ability to take it.

Numbers 13:30-33 (NLT) - 30 But Caleb tried to quiet the people as they stood before Moses. "Let's go at once to take the land," he said. "We can certainly conquer it!"

31 But the other men who had explored the land with him disagreed. "We can't go up against them! They are stronger than we are!"

32 So they spread this bad report about the land among the Israelites: "The land we traveled through and explored will devour anyone who goes to live there. All the people we saw were huge.

33 We even saw giants there, the descendants of Anak. Next to them we felt like grasshoppers, and that's what they thought, too!"

Not only did these people believe an evil report, they also accepted a new genetic makeup that God had never called or given to them. In verse 33, the leaders announced to the people how they felt being in the presence of their "enemies". They announced that they felt like grasshoppers and that's what their enemy thought of them too. How unimaginable! How absurd! They took on the identity of a grasshopper.

Forty years later, when the children of the murmuring generation did prepare to take the promised land, they found out that the people of the land were terribly afraid of them and had been afraid for forty years.

Joshua 2:8-11 (AMP) - 8 Now before the two men lay down [to sleep], Rahab came up to them on the roof,

9 and she said to the men, "I know that the Lord has given you the land, and that the terror and dread of you has fallen on us, and that all the inhabitants of the land have melted [in despair] because of you.

10 For we have heard how the Lord dried up the water of the [a]Red Sea for you when you came out of Egypt, and what you did to the two kings of the Amorites who were beyond the Jordan [on the east], to Sihon and Og, whom you utterly destroyed.

11 When we heard it, our hearts melted [in despair], and a [fighting] spirit no longer remained in any man because of you; for the Lord your God, He is God in heaven above and on earth beneath.

At any time if that murmuring generation would have given up their bad attitude of defeat and repented, they could have taken the promised land God had planned for them. Instead, they chose to lay down and die. They used their voices to pronounce death and got it.

Numbers 14:26-32 (NLT) - 26 Then the Lord said to Moses and Aaron,

27 "How long must I put up with this wicked community and its complaints about me? Yes, I have heard the complaints the Israelites are making against me.

28 Now tell them this: 'As surely as I live, declares the Lord, I will do to you the very things I heard you say.

29 You will all drop dead in this wilderness! Because you complained against me, every one of you who is twenty years old or older and was included in the registration will die.

30 You will not enter and occupy the land I swore to give you. The only exceptions will be Caleb son of Jephunneh and Joshua son of Nun.

31 "'You said your children would be carried off as plunder. Well, I will bring them safely into the land, and they will enjoy what you have despised.

32 But as for you, you will drop dead in this wilderness.

Continuous complaining against God and His plan for the Israelites produced results that were not intended by God. God's plan was for them to go from Egypt through the wilderness and to the promised land. That simple! They complicated it with unbelief!

Your life and the call of God on your life has been intricately planned before the foundations of the world.

Jeremiah 1:5 (NLT) - 5 "I knew you before I formed you in your mother's womb. Before you were born I set you apart and appointed you as my prophet to the nations."

Don't stop, complicate, or dismiss God's plan with your unbelief. How does unbelief manifest itself? It manifests through disobedience. When you say "yes" to God but in your heart you don't really trust Him fully, that's disobedience. It's not that you don't know what to do, it's that you don't believe you can do what God asked you to do. That, my friend, is a wicked report. It's taking God's plan and reporting wickedly on it. It's saying God's plan, the one He prepared for you to do before He formed you, is flawed. You are saying God's choice of you is a joke. You are mishandling God's Kingdom design. Wow!

Don't be dismayed if you've been ignoring God's request of you. I want you to stop and consider this question: What was the last instruction God gave you? How did you respond? Whatever it was, if you responded with a "no," or murmured about it, then take a moment now and repent. Ask God to forgive your unbelief and to return you to a right place in

Him. Ask Him to return you to the place that you can say "yes" to His plan instead of having your children have to fulfill what you refuse to do. God is the restorer and redeemer of time. He can bring you back into the place you need to be. Thank God!

CHAPTER 3

Restoring The Marred Identity

When you don't know your true identity, you are more vulnerable to change your ways to please people. Your identity is not just about your purpose, but it is about the spiritual, physical and mental components that make up who you are. It is the way you think, respond and relate to people. It is your unique connection with the world around you. You are the only person that can be you. Your identity gives you access to the places God designed for you to occupy.

Who you are provides the framework for your existence on earth. It corresponds to the purpose God designed you to fulfill. If your identity is damaged, then your purpose is hindered. This is why it is very important for you to protect who you are. It is important to protect your heart from people who are more interested in hurting your future than helping you to fulfill it.

But what if you were disfigured before you could even determine who you were? What if you were abused and misused by those who were supposed to be your protectors or trainers in the things that God wants you to do? What happens to you? There is still hope, - there is always hope. I want you to know that it is your own willful actions of denial of God's plan that forfeits your entrance into God purpose, not the forceful actions of others.

Your personal opinion of yourself may have been marred with scenes of insecurity and inadequacy because of what was done to you or what you've been told about yourself. The rituals of self-inflicted humiliation may have been the daily routine of your upbringing, but no more! You are free through Christ to live in all that God has called you to be. You will live to be and do all that God has planned for you. Make the decision to start now!

So where do you start? You may be wondering how to figure out your true identity. Your identity may have been suppressed by abuse and lack of knowledge. Just being alive now may be a big feat for you to have accomplished. Let me tell you, your life now is not in vain. You have conquered and survived this long to share with the world your true identity and make the mark God intended for you to make.

Today, you may think that on the outside people see you as a successful, happy, go-getter. They may admire your tenacity and your ability to grab life by the horns. But, privately you think of yourself as not good enough, not as perfect as you ought to be, or not talented enough to do what you would really like to do. You don't have to feel this way any longer. You can know who you are and why you were created like you were.

If you keep living a life where privately you feel differently than the public image you display, you will build confusion and chaos in your mind. The difference between the two images of who you are will develop a habit of self-inflicted defeat in your life that will affect your perception and belief in who you are in everything you do. Because of the constant barraging of thoughts you maintain about your shortcomings, you are developing a resume of why you are not qualified for anything God may ask you to do. You will behave as if God only sees what you present in public, when in fact He sees who you really think you are. He sees what's in your heart.

1 Samuel 16:7 (AMP)- 7 But the Lord said to Samuel, "Do not look at his appearance or at the height of his stature, because I have rejected him. For the Lord sees not as man sees; for man looks [a]at the outward appearance, but the Lord looks at the heart."

Let's examine the concept of what God sees for a moment. Which part of you do you really believe God sees? Do you think He only sees what you are showing Him or others? Or do you know and realize that He sees everything, both what you expose and what you withhold. None of it is hidden from Him, yet, He asks you to participate in His Kingdom plan on earth anyway.

Jeremiah 23:24 (AMP) - 24 "Can anyone hide himself in secret places. So that I cannot see him?" says the Lord. "Do I not fill heaven and earth?" says the Lord.

Psalm 139:7-8 (NLT) - 7 I can never escape from your Spirit! I can never get away from your presence! 8 If I go up to heaven, you are there; if I go down to the grave,[a] you are there.

As Jeremiah and the psalmist realized, God knows everything that pertains to you. He even knows what other people really think about you and if they are lifting you up or pulling you down wrongfully. He doesn't look to anyone else's opinion of you to make His decisions about you and the plan He predesigned for you. God knows what He created you to be and do and He sees what you're actually doing. He knows both your shortcomings and your victories. He knows it all. Instead of thinking of yourself as unqualified the next time God gives you an assignment, rejoice because God has approved of you to do something for Him, in spite of what He already knows about you.

What higher compliment and acceptance can we hope for than when God calls us into His service? He is the King of kings and Lord of lords, the Creator of the universe and mankind. He is the Alpha and Omega, and He is love. This is the character and qualification of the One who has considered you worthy and valuable to do His work for His Kingdom. Amazing!

Understanding God's Identity

In the same light, you must also understand what God is not. God is not a man. If you can grasp the concept that God is not a man, but He is God, this will release you from thinking that God thinks of you as man thinks of you. Why is this important? Man is a created being and Satan, your enemy, is also a created being. If you think of Satan and God in the same level or having the same right to their opinion of you, then you are placing God at the same level of a being He created. Likewise, if you take man's opinion instead of God's opinion, which is the truth, you put God's opinion as equal to man's. This will never be true in any age to come. God's thoughts are always higher and His ways are always greater than ours. Mere man cannot comprehend the plans that God has for you. Satan can't even fathom the greatness you can achieve through the power of God in your life.

1 Corinthians 2:9 (NLT) - 9 That is what the Scriptures mean when they say, "No eye has seen, no ear has heard, and no mind has imagined what God has prepared for those who love him."

Not only does this verse show us that man cannot comprehend what God has in store for us, it also shows us a key to getting out from under any words or actions of the enemy's attempts to hinder our identity. This key is found at the end of the verse, "for those who love Him." Those who love God are capable of receiving what God has in store for them. What God has in store for us is higher and greater than any created being can understand. Neither man nor Satan can comprehend the vastness of what God has in store for us to do on this earth.

God tells us in Numbers, that He is not a man that He should lie. God does not have to impress anyone. He is God. Therefore, He has no desire to lie to you to get His way. With that said, if God asks you to do something, He is not lying to you to help you feel better about yourself; instead, He is pulling out of you the abilities and gifts that He put in you when He created you for this earth. Let's look closer at the verse in Numbers.

Numbers 23:19 (AMP) -19 - "God is not a man, that He should lie, Nor a son of man, that He should repent. Has He said, and will He not do it? Or has He spoken and will He not make it good and fulfill it?

In this verse we see the identity of God revealed to us. He is not a man. He is not a liar. He does not have to repent. He will do what He says. He will fulfill anything that He has spoken. These are all characteristics of God's identity that we see in this verse.

Now, what type of reservations could you possibly have of someone with such high caliber and character? What kind of skepticism do you feel about someone who is so perfect? Can you handle the truth that God is perfect, that He is not a man, and that He never lies? You see, until this truth settles in your spirit as absolute, rigid, unmovable, and unchangeable, you will not be able to believe that what God says about you is true. You will not believe that what God asks you to do is the right fit or the right thing for you to do. You will not be able to think yourself "worthy" of such a position or task.

Understanding and accepting God's identity is one of the most important pieces of information you must possess. This will determine the difference between life or death for you. Knowing God's identity holds the clues and the foundation for discovering your own identity.

If we lack knowledge about who God is, we lack a fulfilling life and run the risk of being destroyed, or worse, ruining our relationship with God.

Hosea 4:6 (NLT) - 6 My people are being destroyed because they don't know me. Since you priests refuse to know me, I refuse to recognize you as my priests. Since you have forgotten the laws of your God, I will forget to bless your children.

We have to remember that the conception and creation of man was thought of and executed by God. He is the one who came up with the idea to create man in the first place. He is the one who created earth for us to live in so that He could spend time with people that looked like and behaved like Him.

Genesis 1:26 (NLT) - 26 Then God said, "Let us make human beings[a] in our image, to be like us. They will reign over the fish in the sea, the birds in the sky, the livestock, all the wild animals on the earth, and the small animals that scurry along the ground."

Psalm 139:14 (KJV) - I will praise thee; for I am fearfully and wonderfully made: marvelous are thy works; and that my soul knoweth right well.

Since we are created in God's image, it is an affront to God and a sin for us to behave like Satan, God's enemy, and a creature that has no likeness or character of God. When we treat Satan differently than God treats him, we are demeaning God's authority in our life. We are exalting ourselves over the image and likeness of God. We are saying to Satan, "God didn't give you a chance, but we will." Shocking statement, I know! But, when we decide to listen to someone that God has told to "shut up and get out", we are giving ear to his grievance against God. In other words, we are putting ourselves in the position of judge between God and Satan. We are reopening a case that has already been settled.

In other words, we are entertaining Satan's explanation of why we should be different than how God created us to operate and function. This may seem harsh or farfetched, but let me explain.

Our creation and existence on this earth is God's will. It is not Satan's will, but God's. Therefore, God alone should get the glory for creating us. In Revelation we see this.

Revelation 4:11 (AMP) - 11"Worthy are You, our Lord and God, to receive the glory and the honor and the power; for You created all things, and because of Your will they exist, and were created and brought into being."

Satan's plan is to "recreate" us into *his* image, an image that represents what it looks like to be stripped of power and kicked out of heaven. Jesus testified in Luke 10:18 that He saw Satan fall from heaven like lightning hitting the earth quickly.

Satan got an everlasting boot from God. There is no chance of Satan ever getting back to his old job in heaven. He will never stand before the presence and glory of God's throne again in the position he was created for. This was all because iniquity was found in him according to *Ezekiel 28:15 (KJV) "Thou wast perfect in thy ways from the day that thou wast created, till iniquity was found in thee".*

Iniquity is another word for sinful behavior or thoughts. This iniquity found in Satan instead of faith is displeasing to God.

Hebrews 11:6 (AMP) - 6 But without faith it is impossible to [walk with God and] please Him, for whoever comes [near] to God must [necessarily] believe that He exists and that He rewards those who [earnestly and diligently] seek Him.

When you think badly of yourself and your gifts and abilities, you are taking glory from God and giving it to God's enemy and yours, Satan. You are removing any faith in God's creation of you, and relying only on what you can hear or see in the moment. You are questioning God's miraculous and glorious creation of who you are. You negate God's plan and embrace the enemy's interpretation of who he thinks you are and what he thinks you're capable of doing.

Your Mindset Will Affect Your Victory

Consider the Biblical story of David and Goliath. It speaks to how embracing the enemy's plan can paralyze you. Goliath conditioned the army of Israel to be who he wanted them to be. He wanted them to be defeated by his army, the Philistines, so he used condemning words to change their mindset about who they were.

1 Samuel 17:8-11 ((KJV) - 8 And he stood and cried unto the armies of Israel, and said unto them, Why are ye come out to set your battle in array? am not I a Philistine, and ye servants to Saul? choose you a man for you, and let him come down to me.
9 If he be able to fight with me, and to kill me, then will we be your servants: but if I prevail against him, and kill him, then shall ye be our servants, and serve us.
10 And the Philistine said, I defy the armies of Israel this day; give me a man, that we may fight together.
11 When Saul and all Israel heard those words of the Philistine, they were dismayed, and greatly afraid.

1 Samuel 17:16 (AMP) - 16 The Philistine [Goliath] came out morning and evening, and took his stand for forty days.

We see here that Goliath decided to paint a picture of what he wanted the army of God to look like. Instead of identifying them as an army that was capable of fighting against him, he called them the servants of Saul (vs 8). He also set the parameters of the battle. He asked for one man to fight against him, *one man*. The battle could have been easily won by the army of Israel had they thought about themselves as an army, instead of servants of Saul. They should have thought of themselves as an army that could fight together and win. Instead, they only thought of sending one man, which was the enemy's suggestion. They listened to the enemy's instruction and disregarded their training as fighters of the army of God.

What has the enemy done in your life to cause you to fight him on his terms? Has he paralyzed you as a solider in God's army? Are you thinking of yourself as part of the army of God or just a weak, burnt out Christian? These are important questions to answer for your own life. If you can't see who God is and on whose side you fight, you will always fall prey to the enemy and his definition of you.

Goliath continued his barrage of undermining the authority and position of God's army, and they continued to accept and agree with it. Don't ever allow the enemy to speak to you about who you are and what you can do. Develop an affront to such speech in your presence, no matter who it comes from. Make the enemy flee your presence as you submit to who God created you to be, and don't bow to the devil's analysis of who you are and what you can do.

James 4:7 (KJV) - 7 Submit yourselves therefore to God. Resist the devil, and he will flee from you.

What the devil does not want you to do, more than anything else, is submit to God. This is seen in Genesis 3 when Satan entered the serpent and questioned Eve's submission to

God's instructions to not eat of a particular tree.

Genesis 3 (KJV) - 3 Now the serpent was more subtil than any beast of the field which the Lord God had made. And he said unto the woman, Yea, hath God said, Ye shall not eat of every tree of the garden?

2 And the woman said unto the serpent, We may eat of the fruit of the trees of the garden:

3 But of the fruit of the tree which is in the midst of the garden, God hath said, Ye shall not eat of it, neither shall ye touch it, lest ye die.

4 And the serpent said unto the woman, Ye shall not surely die:

What if God had not told her that she would die if she ate of the tree? Did He have to tell her the consequence, or could He have just kept that to Himself and wait for them to fail? He could have, but God can't help but give us what we need to obey Him. This is how love operates. Love sets us up to win and never to see if we will fail.

Eve's allegiance should have been to God's command not, her escaping from the consequence of disobeying His command. Because she thought of avoiding the consequence instead of obeying God, the enemy could tempt her by lying about how "wrong" God's consequence of disobedience was. By getting Eve to think this way, Satan won.

How did Satan win? By refocusing her attention. I believe that before Satan's conversation with Eve, she probably only thought of not eating of the tree. After his conversation with her, she focused on the impossibility of death from eating of the tree. That focus came from her enemy, not her Creator and Father, God.

What lies has the enemy told you about your identity and obeying God's instructions? Has he told you it's no big deal if you don't do what God asks? Maybe you argue that you're busy, you've been abused, or that you never had opportunities to develop the skills needed, and you think these reasons make you justified to be disobedient to God. But no disobedience to God is ever justified by any excuse man can offer.

Goliath's defiance of God's army met its match when David showed up. David did not bow to Goliath's brainwashing of the army. Instead, he defied the language and stance of Goliath.

1 Samuel 17:26 (AMP) - 26 Then David spoke to the men who were standing by him, "What will be done for the man who kills this Philistine and removes the disgrace [of his taunting] from Israel? For who is this uncircumcised Philistine that he has taunted and defied the armies of the living God?"

David's words about Goliath were not filled with awe or fear. They were filled with disgust. "For who is this uncircumcised Philistine?" David asked the right question about the situation. He asked about the reward for taking down this unqualified enemy, and he asked who this enemy was that he thought he could defy the armies of God. David's perspective on the identities of everyone involved was correct. He called the army the armies of the living God, not the servants of Saul. He called God the living God, not a myth or a joke. He called the enemy, Goliath, as uncircumcised, or a non-covenant partner with the living God.

David spent time worshiping God, he was in awe and had great respect for Him. Therefore, when he heard the lies that were being spoken against God, he responded immediately to shut them down.

What do you do when you hear lies about God? Do you allow people to lie about God's identity and power in your presence by keeping silent? These are important questions to answer for your own life. They hold the key to your ability to trust God with your life. If you're not willing to protect God's Word, power, and call in your life, then you're not ready to trust Him with your life.

If you can't trust God with your life, you will bow to the enemy's plan for the self preservation of who you think you are. A principle to remember is this: if you don't respect someone's authority in your life, you will never respect their instructions to you. God should be the ultimate authority in your life. He should be without doubt the person you say "yes" to no matter the circumstance or the counsel of man. The Bible helps us with this in the book of Romans.

Romans 3:4 (NLT) - 4 Of course not! Even if everyone else is a liar, God is true. As the Scriptures say about him, "You will be proved right in what you say, and you will win your case in court."

Your goal today is to obey God's instructions to you over and above man's expectations of you. Don't be shy about disobeying what man wants in order to obey what God says. God will back you up!

FIONA PYSZKA

CHAPTER 4

Know The Word, Walk In Faith

There are things that could have happened in your life to cause your identity to be marred. These actions can undoubtedly cause ruin and chaos in your soul and spirit. However, there is an even greater issue that could hold you back: the issue of lack of knowledge.

Lack of knowledge is when we don't know truths that exist. When you are unaware of the truths that exist, lies can plague your life. Just because truth exists does not mean it is working on your behalf. We see in the book of Hosea where people die for what they don't know, not because a solution to their problem doesn't exist.

Hosea 4:6 - My people are destroyed for lack of knowledge [of My law, where I reveal My will]. Because you [the priestly nation] have rejected knowledge, I will also reject you from being My priest. Since you have forgotten the law of your God, I will also forget your children.

As you can see from this verse, the consequences for living day to day with a lack of knowledge does not affect just you, it also affects your children. When your children are affected, their children will be affected and now a cycle has been created. Think of what things keep happening generation after generation in your family life. Is there a particular repeat of the same problem in at least one family member?

Whenever you see this pattern, whether in your family or another, realize that there is a truth unknown. When there is a truth unknown, there is lack of knowledge.

The best and most helpful knowledge to possess is the knowledge of God's Word. You need to know what God's Word says about you, your family, your relationship with God, and your enemy. These are critical things to understand from God's Word, because His Word is the only absolute truth. This truth is the best foundation on which to build any relationship on.

God's Word

God's Word was written just for you and me. One of the main reasons for God's Word is to help us live successful lives here on earth. You are not expected to live by God's Word because He is on an ego trip. No! His Word is to be lived by because it provides life and power.

Hebrews 4:12 (AMP) - 12 For the word of God is living and active and full of power [making it operative, energizing, and effective]. It is sharper than any two-edged [a]sword, penetrating as far as the division of the soul and spirit [the completeness of a person], and of both joints and marrow [the deepest parts of our nature], exposing and judging the very thoughts and intentions of the heart.

The Word of God has energizing power. It has life, it hits the mark, and it has answers. God's Word is full of light and life. There is no darkness in what God says. He is clear and plain yet He has many dimensions and levels that we can get to know and understand. The best way to start knowing God is to know His Word. He has written instructions and strategies in His Word to help us live a successful life.

There is no greater way to understand your present, past, or future, than to look to the Word of God. Examples of how we should live are found in the written Word of God. The lives of those who walked before you are displayed for you to analyze so you can avoid their traps and duplicate their winning strategies. These are all things that can be found in the Word of God. But the Bible is not God's only method of speaking to us. John 14:26 shows us that Holy Spirit can also teach us.

John 14:26 (AMP) - 26 But the [a]Helper (Comforter, Advocate, Intercessor—Counselor, Strengthener, Standby), the Holy Spirit, whom the Father will send in My name [in My place, to represent Me and act on My behalf], He will teach you all things. And He will help you remember everything that I have told you.

God also uses men and women to communicate truth about Himself through teaching and preaching the gospel.

Ephesians 4:11-14 (AMP) - 11 And [His gifts to the church were varied and] He Himself appointed some as apostles [special messengers, representatives], some as prophets [who speak a new message from God to the people], some as evangelists [who spread the good news of salvation], and some as pastors and teachers [to shepherd and guide and instruct],

12 [and He did this] to fully equip and perfect the saints (God's people) for works of service, to build up the body of Christ [the church];

13 until we all reach oneness in the faith and in the knowledge of the Son of God, [growing spiritually] to become a mature believer, reaching to the measure of the fullness of Christ [manifesting His spiritual completeness and exercising our spiritual gifts in unity].

14 So that we are no longer children [spiritually immature], tossed back and forth [like ships on a stormy sea] and carried about by every wind of [shifting] doctrine, by the cunning and trickery of [unscrupulous] men, by the deceitful scheming of people ready to do anything [for personal profit].

We see God has set up offices with different giftings that will help you fulfill and discover your identity and what you should do as a child of God. Verse 14 shows us a picture of why we need people who are equipped to help us. We need to grow up and be mature Christians. No matter your natural age, your spiritual age can be different. For example, you may be an adult who just received Jesus as Savior. If that's the case, you are a baby Christian. You need to be nourished on the Word of God to help you grow and mature. Or, you may be a teenager who has been a Christian your whole life. If you have been feeding on God's Word, then you may be more spiritually mature than the adult who just received Salvation.

Whatever the case, every Christian, no matter how mature, needs to feed continually on the Word of God to grow in the knowledge of God's Word and thus increase their maturity in being who God created them to be.

A lack of knowledge of God's Word will keep you from growing and receiving the benefits of being a part of the Kingdom of God. Without the knowledge of God's Word, you could very well live under the curse of the kingdom of darkness.

Galatians 3:13 (NLT) - 13 But Christ has rescued us from the curse pronounced by the law. When he was hung on the cross, he took upon himself the curse for our wrongdoing. For it is written in the Scriptures, "Cursed is everyone who is hung on a tree."

Lacking knowledge could wrongfully enslave you to the curse of the law because you still want to succeed by your own works instead of faith in God's Word. Jesus' blood on the cross was shed so that you don't have to walk and live in this curse anymore. Knowing the Word of God on overcoming the curse will take you further than you could ever go on your own, because faith comes by hearing and hearing the Word (see Romans 10:17).

In my own life, I grew up as a church girl and thought I knew a lot about the Bible. After all, I had been a Sunday School teacher, church treasurer, and most qualified of all, a preacher's kid. However, none of these "church" positions helped me increase in the knowledge of God. Only God's Word can do that. When I first encountered teaching that taught me what the redemption of Christ paid for, I was shocked and excited. I couldn't believe what I didn't know about God. I was taken aback that I had known God my whole life but never knew basic things I should have known about Him and about the benefits of being born again.

Maybe you find yourself in the same situation. You've been a Christian for a long time and still may be surprised by some of what I'm sharing. Don't be discouraged about what you should have known; be encouraged that you get to learn it now. Take it all in, and be like a sponge soaking in the training from God's Word. His Word is quick and powerful. It can do things that no other word or tool can do. Here is a reminder of what He said about His Word.

Hebrews 4:12 (NLT) - 12 For the word of God is alive and powerful. It is sharper than the sharpest two-edged sword, cutting between soul and spirit, between joint and marrow. It exposes our innermost thoughts and desires.

Let the Word of God expose thoughts in your life that have been holding you back from believing completely in God and His Word.

Faith

The Word of God is so powerful that it can fix any problem in your life. The key to working the Word of God in your life is to use the faith that comes from hearing the Word.

Romans 10:17 (KJV)- 17 So then faith cometh by hearing, and hearing by the word of God.

Faith is key to observing and allowing the Word of God to work for you. If you speak God's Word in prayer or as a confession over your life, and it is not done with your belief that it will happen despite what you feel or see, then you're not using that scripture in faith.

Don't beat yourself up if this is what you've been doing. Instead, just adjust your sails and start heading in the right direction. There is no time with God; everything about God is *now*. So He can get answers to you in any time frame you have to work with.

More importantly, the Bible tells us that faith is *now*. This means that once believed faith works immediately. You can activate faith in your life for any situation at any time.

Hebrews 11:1 (AMP) - 11 Now faith is the assurance (title deed, confirmation) of things hoped for (divinely guaranteed), and the evidence of things not seen [the conviction of their reality—faith comprehends as fact what cannot be experienced by the physical senses].

But, how do you have faith ready to work when you need it? This is a very important question to answer and understand for the rest of your life. Developing faith should be your job in every season. When life is going great and there's no reason to use "emergency" prayers or faith, you should be developing your faith account so that you have reserves to pull from. You will have such an overflowing account that you have faith to assist your neighbor. You need to live by faith every day.

Faith building is simply hearing for yourself the Word of God, believing everything you hear of the Word of God, and acting it out every day. That's it! That's how strong faith is developed. Weak faith happens when fear comes in and tells you that no such thing exists as *all truth*. No one is true 100% of the time. That's what fear embeds in the minds of people to create just a seed of doubt about what God says or wants to do for them.

Focus on reading God's Word and saying out loud, "Yes Lord, I agree with what this says." Even if you don't understand it yet, just agree with it. It's amazing the results you will have in developing your faith and walking by faith. Next time you need to use faith, you will find yourself saying, "Why couldn't it be done?" instead of "Could it really be done?"

A great way to put this into practice is to make a list of

subject areas that you would like to see impacted with your words and actions. Things that you would like to see results in when you pray. Maybe your list would look like this:

1. Health

2. Finances

3. Strong Marriage/Finding a Spouse

4. Having Children/Raising Children

5. Career Choice

6. Purpose in life

7. Miracles, Signs, Wonders

What's the problem that plagues your life? What thing do you constantly say you could have if only you were good enough? Maybe it has nothing to do with your good works; maybe it has to do with how much you believe God's Word. That could simply be the *only* thing that's holding things up.

One way that we show disbelief of God's Word is to say or think that if God *cared* He would have answered us or done something about our problem. Jesus encountered that with His disciples.

Mark 4:38-41 (AMP) - 38 But Jesus was in the stern, asleep [with His head] on the [sailor's leather] cushion. And they woke Him and said to Him, "Teacher, do You not care that we are about to die?" 39 And He got up and [sternly] rebuked the wind and said to the sea, "Hush, be still (muzzled)!" And the wind died down [as if it had grown weary] and there was [at once] a great calm [a perfect peacefulness]. 40 Jesus said to them, "Why are you afraid? Do you still have no faith and confidence [in Me]?" 41 They were filled with great fear, and said to each other, "Who then is this, that even the wind and the sea obey Him?"

What the disciples didn't realize is that the wind and the waves would have obeyed them also. They just did not use faith to command the storm to stop. That's it! Jesus was awakened to do what they had the power to do. They just needed to use faith. It was not a matter of not having the same power Jesus had; it was about not having enough faith.

What excuses have you found yourself making lately concerning the things you're expecting God to do for you? Maybe there's something you want to stop. Well, like the wind and waves had to obey Jesus' voice, your storm can obey your voice too.

Only you must speak to it and not blame God for it not stopping. Don't describe the storm to all of your friends. You have to speak to it. Don't take it in as a pet. Rebuke it like the thief that it is. Do it quickly as if your life depends on it, because it does!

When you're in a battle for your life, don't just look for people to pat you on the back or give you "encouraging" words. Look for those who will fight with you to win over the enemy that is attacking you. Faith is how you overcome. The fight of faith is the fight that wins.

1 John 5:4 (KJV) - 4 For whatsoever is born of God overcometh the world: and this is the victory that overcometh the world, even our faith.

1 Timothy 6:12 (KJV) - 12 Fight the good fight of faith, lay hold on eternal life, whereunto thou art also called, and hast professed a good profession before many witnesses.

Preserving your identity, who God created you to be, requires a fight of faith. Don't just sit back and let the enemy walk all over you, derailing your future with different tactics that you accept as punishment for the sin or sins you may have committed. Mistakes of your past do not have to ruin the great joy that God has prepared for your future. To get back on track you must build your faith so that you can walk with confidence in your faith.

What does walking in your faith look like? Jesus often rebuked those who did not walk in faith against what was happening to them or around them. Consider the story of Peter walking on water in Matthew 14:29-31. Peter saw something he never saw before and was wondering if it could be Jesus or not. In today's terminology we would probably ask whether what we're seeing is of God or not. In order to find out if it was really Jesus, Peter asked Jesus, "If it is You, tell me to come." Jesus told Peter, "Come." Peter stepped out of the boat and came towards Jesus. However, Peter was not ready for the environment in which Jesus' faith was working. Peter's faith was not ready to follow through with Jesus' instruction completely. In the storm, Peter failed to walk in faith.

Peter was desperate to walk in the things that Jesus walked in. He wanted to be like Jesus. How many people today, yourself included, want to be just like Jesus was when He walked this earth? One of the things about Jesus was that no matter what scenario He was faced with, He never lost His identity. He knew who He was, and He knew who God said He was.

When we are not sure of what God thinks about us, we start trying to do things to impress God to show Him that we are good enough to be His child. God already accepted you as His child when you repented from being a sinner and He forgave you. That's when you became a child of God. Now to please Him, you just have to walk by faith in your life.

Hebrews 11:6 (KJV) - 6 But without faith it is impossible to please him: for he that cometh to God must believe that he is, and that he is a rewarder of them that diligently seek him.

No matter how hard you try, if you don't have faith in God and who He is, you will never please Him. So instead of spending your time thinking of how much God couldn't possibly do something for little ole you, start spending your time meditating (thinking over and over about) on God's Word and see what you will start believing.

For example, here is how Mary responded when she was asked to carry Jesus in her womb.

Luke 1:38 (NLT) - 38 Mary responded, "I am the Lord's servant. May everything you have said about me come true." And then the angel left her.

She did not understand how she could conceive since the normal way required a man's participation. She'd never known a man in such a way, so she was puzzled. But in this moment of not understanding the process, she still believed the One who asked the question.

Wow! What an amazing response. What a powerful, confident response in who God said Mary was. If you read the encounter between her and the angel, you will find that the angel explained what God wanted her to do and answered her question. After that, she joyfully accepted her assignment and completely agreed with what God said. She accepted her God-given identity.

Mary's choice had an impact on Joseph's life too. But she made the bold choice to choose God's plans for her not just what was right for her family or culture. She was not afraid to say "Yes God, I am Your servant". Her bold decision affected the world. Wow!

How about you today? Are you spending your life finding ways in which to tell God about your inability to be who He says you are and to do what He's asked you to do? Are you speaking to God things contrary to what He's speaking to you?

CHAPTER 5

Offense Hurts Your Identity

Being offended has become a plague in today's culture. There is hardly a day that goes by that you do not read or hear about a person or people group offended at what was done against them. Division among people is how the enemy can come in and give you a vision for life that pulls down instead of builds up. Remember, you were created by the same God that created someone who looks, speaks, and behaves completely different than you. That's God's model. Freedom to make choices is what makes us human. The key is to not be offended at someone's choices that you don't agree with.

The enemy's best tool to accomplish the task of pulling you down is offense. Offense shows up in different shades depending on where in the world you are. It also has a different approach for the cultural or spiritual roots you participate in. When you realize the reason for offense and the deadly consequences it produces, you will stay far from it. Knowing how destructive offense is will compel you to make a decision to fix your heart on the matter, no matter how hard someone tries to thrust in your face their disapproval of you.

How can you pull off such a big feat? It's simple! Know who

you are. When you know who you are, any other label won't make you angry; it will make you laugh. The problem arises when you don't know who you are. If you don't know who you are and someone labels you with a "bad" label, you react harshly because you don't like their label, and because you don't know how to express who you really are. So, you put up a fight to prove that the label they're giving you is not right. However you don't know what is right. Even if you think you know, you're still not sure, so you get defensive.

Defensiveness is a default position taken to protect any perceived attack. The problem with responding defensively against an attack on your life or your belief system is that it requires no faith in God's Word, only protection of your word. John 8 shows how Jesus reacted to wrong words about Him.

John 8:14-19 (NLT) - 14 Jesus told them, "These claims are valid even though I make them about myself. For I know where I came from and where I am going, but you don't know this about me.

15 You judge me by human standards, but I do not judge anyone.

16 And if I did, my judgment would be correct in every respect because I am not alone. The Father who sent me is with me.

17 Your own law says that if two people agree about something, their witness is accepted as fact.

18 I am one witness, and my Father who sent me is the other."

19 "Where is your father?" they asked.

Jesus answered, "Since you don't know who I am, you don't know who my Father is. If you knew me, you would also know my Father."

If you notice here, Jesus did not respond to them according

to their human standards of judgment. He addressed who He was and revealed their lack of knowledge of God. Jesus did not create a scene and neither did He tell them that He would never speak to them again because they didn't understand Him. No, He simply responded with His identity. That's how you win without being offended: you present your identity. "Take it or leave it, this is who I am and it's not changing." Who you are should be who God says you are and not what life circumstances have made you. Once you are clear about this, then this is the identity that you present in your defense. Never waver when speaking to others about yourself. Never entertain thoughts that contradict your identity. 2 Corinthians 10:5 tells us to take thoughts captive, and thoughts that go against the identity God gave you should always be number one on your list.

James talks about wavering and the results it yields. If you don't stop wavering about your identity, then your efforts to live a successful life will be in vain.

James 1:5-8 (NLT) - 5 If you need wisdom, ask our generous God, and he will give it to you. He will not rebuke you for asking.

6 But when you ask him, be sure that your faith is in God alone. Do not waver, for a person with divided loyalty is as unsettled as a wave of the sea that is blown and tossed by the wind.

7 Such people should not expect to receive anything from the Lord. 8 Their loyalty is divided between God and the world, and they are unstable in everything they do.

The Apostle Paul was a good example of not wavering on who he was. He always said who he was based on who God called him to be. He presented his identity to the courts of earth, and it was verified by the courts of heaven. When you are aligned with heaven about who you are and what you are created to do, God's power will back you up. As a believer of Christ, you have the power to bind and loose things between heaven and earth. You have been given that power by Jesus' work on the cross.

Matthew 18:18 (NLT)- 18 "I tell you the truth, whatever you forbid on earth will be forbidden in heaven, and whatever you permit on earth will be permitted in heaven.

Paul understood this power that has been given to believers. In one place, Paul was almost worshiped as God because of the tremendous power that he demonstrated. When we are hooked into God fully and walking in our true identity, then great exploits are accomplished.

Acts 28:3-6 (NLT) - 3 As Paul gathered an armful of sticks and was laying them on the fire, a poisonous snake, driven out by the heat, bit him on the hand.

4 The people of the island saw it hanging from his hand and said to each other, "A murderer, no doubt! Though he escaped the sea, justice will not permit him to live."

5 But Paul shook off the snake into the fire and was unharmed.

6 The people waited for him to swell up or suddenly drop dead. But when they had waited a long time and saw that he wasn't harmed, they changed their minds and decided he was a god.

What do people see when something "bad" happens in your life? Do they see you shaking it off because you know the power of God, or do they see and hear you grumbling and murmuring against God? This determines the difference in results between the Israelites in the wilderness and the

Christians of the book of Acts. Those who were leaders in the book of Acts accepted the demonstration and power of God as something to be shared and replicated wherever they went. Whereas, the tribal leaders of the Israelites, always doubted what God wanted to do for them next. They always thought they were the grasshoppers of the bunch and that they were going to be taken advantage of. Isn't that the same "logical" description people have of life events today?

When someone has gone through hard times, we expect them to have issues and mistrust with God. Well, that's not how God sees it. He still holds them to His high standards that are still true today. God wants us to trust Him and obey His instructions, not to elevate His ego, but to save our lives.

God does not ask you to "get over" issues without providing support. Here is what Jude had to say about the many issues that were plaguing society in his time.

Jude 17-22 (NLT) - 17 But you, my dear friends, must remember what the apostles of our Lord Jesus Christ predicted.

18 They told you that in the last times there would be scoffers whose purpose in life is to satisfy their ungodly desires.

19 These people are the ones who are creating divisions among you. They follow their natural instincts because they do not have God's Spirit in them.

20 But you, dear friends, must build each other up in your most holy faith, pray in the power of the Holy Spirit,

21 and await the mercy of our Lord Jesus Christ, who will bring you eternal life. In this way, you will keep yourselves safe in God's love.

22 And you must show mercy to those whose faith is wavering.

We see in verses 20 to 21 what our part is in the body of Christ. Our responsibility is to build each other up. We must show mercy to those who have wavering faith. The concept of sowing and reaping is all over the Bible, and we would be wise to consider it in all aspects of our life. If you create a lifestyle of living like one who sows God's Word and practices it with those around you, then when it's time for you to get help, it won't be something you have to "borrow" from someone else. Instead, it will be something that you have planted and can now reap its benefits. You will have a harvest of mercy stored up to help you in your time of wavering or distress.

If however, you practice living a life of offense and always being a victim to the latest drama playing in the theatre of life, you will never have a harvest to pull from. You will always be begging people to pray for you and hoping that their prayers work because you may feel like God is not listening to you (by the way, that is more drama). You are better than this. You are well able to speak to God and hear what He has to say to you. It doesn't matter how young a Christian you are, hearing God can happen right away.

Think of a baby, it takes just moments for a baby to recognize the voice of family members. Especially if mom is on the scene all the time. The baby will recognize the mom's voice no matter where in the room it is coming from. You can have that kind of relationship with God. He knows your name and the sound of your voice. Whether you realize it or not, you also know the voice of God. Here is what Jesus said about the subject.

John 10:26-27 (AMPC) - 26 But you do not believe and trust and rely on Me because you do not belong to My fold [you are no sheep of Mine].

27 The sheep that are My own hear and are listening to My voice; and I know them, and they follow Me.

Confess this Scripture to renew your mind to the truth so you can hear God's voice. Because you may not have known the power of hearing God's voice, you may find it difficult or think that you're not good enough for God to speak to you. Well according to the words of Jesus as shared in John, being good enough is not what qualifies you to hear God's voice. It's whether you're His sheep or not that qualifies you.

Being His sheep is all about accepting Him as your shepherd. He is the great Shepherd. There is none greater. He knows exactly what you need and how to get it to you, according to Psalm 23.

Psalm 23 - 1 The Lord is my shepherd; I have all that I need.

2 He lets me rest in green meadows; he leads me beside peaceful streams.

3 He renews my strength. He guides me along right paths, bringing honor to his name.

God spoke about Himself in the Psalms here, and He demonstrated His leadership as Shepherd in the New Testament. Jesus showed us what a good shepherd looks like and how He takes care of the sheep.

Some of the things Jesus did brought about a no-deficit lifestyle for believers. He healed the sick, raised the dead, cast out demons, and set captives free. He even told the people in church ahead of time that this is what he was going to demonstrate to them while He was here.

Luke 4:17- (AMP)- 17 The scroll of the prophet Isaiah was handed to Him. He unrolled the scroll and found the place where it was written,

18 "The Spirit of the Lord is upon Me (the Messiah),Because He has anointed Me to preach the good news to the poor. He has sent Me to announce release (pardon, forgiveness) to the captives, And recovery of sight to the blind, To set free those who are oppressed (downtrodden, bruised, crushed by tragedy),

19 to proclaim the favorable year of the Lord [the day when salvation and the favor of God abound greatly]."

Jesus laid out for the "church" group who He was and what He was able to do because of the anointing of God. Jesus knew His identity and where His power came from. He also announced it to the right audience before He performed the work. He left no questions about who He was and what power He used, yet they still got offended when He demonstrated who He was.

What can you learn from this? People will be offended whether you're perfect or not. An offended heart will always take offense as a response to anything new. If you are bringing freshness and life to a scene, prepare to be misunderstood and to offend someone. The key is, do not be offended yourself. This will damage your identity, which damages vision.

See clearly, and live an offense-free life. Keep the love of God always flowing through your heart. Give people the benefit of the doubt. Assume they are going on wrong information and don't know the truth about you, that's why they are making things up. Always defer to the good instead of thinking evil. Most of all, leave them in the hands of God for justice. After all, God does know why they are doing it, and He can take care of business for you.

Your position should always be to live in the identity and purpose God has for you. You must walk in who He created you to be. Every time a layer of how you function is revealed, grab it, own it and walk in it.

CHAPTER 6

Identity Crisis

There is an epidemic plaguing society today. It is the confusion of one's identity. You can call it an identity crisis of epic proportions. It is so tragic that the media and society's elite are finding it difficult to reward people who fight wars, invent lifesaving tools or negotiate peace treaties. Instead, they find themselves praising those with the "courage" to rewire their physical body, changing from man to woman.

The changing of one's gender seems to be the hottest ticket to fame and adoration in this culture. Media and professionals are being commended for giving a voice to this chaotic distortion of God's creation of man. This is a really big problem that today's generation faces. It would be nice if this crisis would go away, be blocked from the airwaves or be put behind the curtain: however, hiding this travesty does not solve the problem. We must get to the root of the matter and determine where this identity confusion comes from.

Confusion, whether in gender identity or career choice, all stem from the same source. It is a place of darkness and hopelessness, where a struggle for importance is a daily fight. Confusion is fostered in an atmosphere of rejection. Where rejection abides, confusion grows. God is not the source of confusion, He is the source of order.

1 Corinthians 14:33 (AMP) - 33 for God [who is the source of their prophesying] is not a God of confusion and disorder but of peace and order. As [is the practice] in all the churches of the saints (God's people),

God does not reject you, but you could reject God. You may not have rejected God altogether, but there may be an area of your life, of your heart, that you are unwilling to allow Him to access. When you refuse to accept God's help, you are rejecting God. God has always been there waiting for you to come to Him. He is not a forceful dictator, and His commands are backed by His support. Your obedience to God's commands secures His support. Your disobedience to God's commands loses His support. It is that simple. God does not force loyalty, but He does present a good case for being loyal to Him.

Psalm 95:7-11 (AMP) - 7 For He is our God. And we are the people of His pasture and the sheep of His hand. Today, if you will hear His voice,

8 Do not harden your hearts and become spiritually dull as at Meribah [the place of strife], And as at Massah [the place of testing] in the wilderness,

9 "When your fathers tested Me, They tried Me, even though they had seen My work [of miracles].

10 "For forty years I was grieved and disgusted with that generation, And I said, 'They are a people who err in their heart, And they do not acknowledge or regard My ways.'

11 "Therefore I swore [an oath] in My wrath, 'They absolutely shall not enter My rest [the land of promise].'"

In verse 10 we see how long God puts up with people that grieve Him. People who do not follow His instructions to them for life, but complain non-stop about what He hasn't done for them and what He could have done better grieve God.

Does that sound familiar to today's epidemic of the complaining, striving, and "it's my right" atmosphere that has sprung up in the world? It has become like weeds in a well maintained garden, waiting to choke out the nutrients from viable plants. Your mind is like a garden. This is why you need to pay attention to what is planted in your mind. Daily you will be bombarded with information through media, friends complaining, or even products in a store. You have to take charge of what stays in your mind and what goes. Immediately you must dismiss thoughts of tolerance and understanding towards things that the Bible deems sin. Do not try to understand why someone feels the need to live sinfully as a lifestyle. Simply denounce it for your own life.

Anything that God has deemed unacceptable to Him should also be unacceptable to us. We are here representing Him and His Kingdom policies, are we not?

Let's take for example the gender identity crisis that plagues the world today. This is a play by the enemy for rampant sin to be committed and accepted as "normal." The sin of homosexuality is not new to the earth: it was happening back in the days of the Bible, and is why the Apostles addressed it in their preaching and explained its stench to the nostrils of God. If the Apostles had just "let it go," people would have continued down a path of self destruction. Their sin would not have affected only them, but their generations to come.

1 Timothy 1:10 (NLT) - 10 The law is for people who are sexually immoral, or who practice homosexuality, or are slave traders, liars, promise breakers, or who do anything else that contradicts the wholesome teaching

In the days of Noah, the world was wiped away with the flood. It was the sinfulness of man and his way of living that stirred up an insatiable appetite for sin that could not be fulfilled. Men desired unholy union with each other.

Genesis 6:11-12 (NLT) - 11 Now God saw that the earth had become corrupt and was filled with violence. 12 God observed all this corruption in the world, for everyone on earth was corrupt.

This lifestyle became so vile that even angels were not exempt from being pursued to satisfy the raving appetite of lustful men and their same-sex attraction. Remember the story of Lot and his family being rescued by angels from Sodom and Gomorrah (see Genesis 19)? Even the intercession of Abraham could not stop God's judgment on the city because of their great sin. Abraham tried, but God could not find enough righteous people to save the city. God wants to save the world, but can He find enough righteous to qualify for the world to be saved? I believe He can. I am willing to be counted as one, are you?

Peace and contentment are God's plan for your life. Even if you are fighting the fight of faith, you can still do it with confidence, joy and peace knowing you will win, because Jesus already won the fight. You are simply enforcing His victory. You are holding and protecting what God already gave to you. Being contented counts as being satisfied with God's plan and not your own fleshly desires.

Philippians 4:11 (NLT) - 11 Not that I was ever in need, for I have learned how to be content with whatever I have.

When you live a life that is content, you are a threat to your enemy. He does not have leverage over you to entice you to mourn after what you don't have. You're too busy using what you do have to bring glory to God. You're not burying your talent, you're investing it so that it can multiply. Let's look at the story in the Bible of the person who thought the money he was asked to invest by his master was not "good enough." What was the master's response?

Matthew 25:24-29 (NLT) - 24 "Then the servant with the one bag of silver came and said, 'Master, I knew you were a harsh man, harvesting crops you didn't plant and gathering crops you didn't cultivate. 25 I was afraid I would lose your money, so I hid it in the earth. Look, here is your money back.'

26 "But the master replied, 'You wicked and lazy servant! If you knew I harvested crops I didn't plant and gathered crops I didn't cultivate, 27 why didn't you deposit my money in the bank? At least I could have gotten some interest on it.'

28 "Then he ordered, 'Take the money from this servant, and give it to the one with the ten bags of silver. 29 To those who use well what they are given, even more will be given, and they will have an abundance. But from those who do nothing, even what little they have will be taken away.

An identity crisis occurs when you compare yourself with other people. It's always about how someone else is doing in life, or how happy someone else is, and how much you're not.

This is not a new trick of your enemy. Remember what he did to Eve. He created a lack in her that didn't exist. He created a desire in her that she had never expressed or talked to Adam about. He showed her the one thing that was keeping her alive forever; he told her that if she messed with it nothing would change. But in fact, it was all a lie. It always is a lie. Whenever the enemy opens his mouth to you, he can only speak lies. *Satan's heart is a casket full of lies.*

The devil wants to create an appetite in you to be the gender you think has it better than the other. If you're a woman, he wants you to feel that men take advantage of you and you will never be promoted, or that you are being mistreated because of a man. That's a lie. Here's what the Bible says about promotion.

Psalm 75:6-7 (KJV) - 6 For promotion cometh neither from the east, nor from the west, nor from the south.

7 But God is the judge: he putteth down one, and setteth up another.

The Bible further shares how women changed the course of history, in spite of how society treated women in that time. Examples of women who made such tremendous exploits for mankind include Deborah the first woman judge, Esther the first orphan queen, Ruth the Moabitess that came into the lineage of Jesus, and Mary the mother of Jesus. All of these were women who changed history and fulfilled God's plan on earth.

If you are a man, the enemy will lie to also. He may deceive you into thinking all financial and leadership responsibilities lie with you for your household. He may tell you that your career is limited to certain field, or that you are to hear from God for all of the women in your life. What a complete and utter trap these thoughts can set for your life. These lies, if believed, can cause you to set up a lifestyle where you can only manage these huge, unreasonable responsibilities by controlling the women in your life. You may not even realize this is what you're doing. Your efforts are simply to hold things together so that the women you are responsible for do not get hurt in some way. Biggest of all, you don't want to disobey God.

Let me help you solve this dilemma. There are no verses in the Bible that ask men to be responsible for all women. A husband is responsible for his wife, and a father for his daughter. Responsibility does not mean you are held accountable for how they think, act or behave. You are responsible for leading them in the things of God, not leading them by telling them what God wants them to do. If you could just understand this principle, it would take a lot of pressure off your shoulders. God wants to speak directly to men and women alike. Hebrews 12 shows us that Jesus mediates between God and all people, not only men.

Hebrews 12:24(NLT) - 24 You have come to Jesus, the one who mediates the new covenant between God and people, and to the sprinkled blood, which speaks of forgiveness instead of crying out for vengeance like the blood of Abel.

He does not want a man to decipher His messages for Him. He doesn't want a woman to tell a man how to do what He wants the man to do.

God wants men and women to work with each other, complimentary and not competitively working together, both achieving God's goals, not culture's expectations. If you expect men to give permission for you to do something, or women to help you fulfill God's requests of you, then you are setting yourself up to depend on other people and not faith in God's Word.

If you don't accept the gender God sent you to earth with, it will be highly unlikely that you can accept anything else He created you to do. Satan knows that in order to dispossess you of your purpose, he needs to rewire everything about you. He needs to make sure you never meet the right spouse and that you hate God enough to never listen to a word He says. Think about it! If you were born a woman and you decide to change your gender to man, you will most likely be marrying a woman. Likewise, if you decide as a woman that you don't like men and you like women sexually, then you will marry a woman. God has never provided the same gender as a spouse for anyone in the Bible, neither did He use a same gender couple to bring forth any child.

Some people with gender confusion may walk around mad at God, accusing Him of "creating" them that way, while others say that God agrees with them. Both of these beliefs about God are false. God did not create anyone's brain to think opposite of their gender. God was not confused when He designed men and women. God is holy. The sinful nature goes against all that God calls holy. It renders God's ways undesirable.

1 Samuel 2:2 (KJV) - 2 There is none holy as the Lord: for there is none beside thee: neither is there any rock like our God.

Galatians 5:19 (NLT) - 19 When you follow the desires of your sinful nature, the results are very clear: sexual immorality, impurity, lustful pleasures,

As a matter of fact, confused thinking is what gets a person more committed to their path of "self-destruction" than what the enemy could personally do to derail them. God's plans for your life could never be stolen by the enemy. Instead, he can only take it from you with your permission. He is a thief, so the way he takes it is robbery, but he cannot enter your house without your permission. He enters as a guest by getting you to open the door. The Bible warns us not to give the devil a foothold.

Ephesians 4:27 (NLT) - 27 for anger gives a foothold to the devil.

You're probably thinking, "why would anyone ever have the devil in their house as a guest?" You may be surprised to know how many have entertained the devil without realizing it. Eve was entertaining a guest in her garden and didn't realize who it was. All the while she probably thought she was talking to the animal God created, not the angel He had kicked out of heaven.

Eve's conversation with Satan gave him her world!

What lies are you allowing in your house? Your mind controls what comes into your house and what is put on a black list, never allowed to enter. Your heart reveals the types of people whose voice you've permitted to control your mind, thus controlling your life. Your heart reveals who you worship.

Luke 6:45 (KJV) - 45 A good man out of the good treasure of his heart bringeth forth that which is good; and an evil man out of the evil treasure of his heart bringeth forth that which is evil: for of the abundance of the heart his mouth speaketh.

Proverbs 23:7A (KJV) - 7 For as he thinketh in his heart, so is he:

Your lifestyle reveals what has been developing in your heart, whether you're a good tree or a bad tree. Psalm 1 tells us what type of person is blessed by God: One that does not take advice from mockers or walks with sinners. A blessed person is one that delights in the law or Word of God. This person, the psalmist says, will be like a tree planted by living waters. A tree planted by the right waters will be fruitful. For a tree to produce fruit it has to be healthy, and a healthy tree knows what fruit it was designed to produce.

Psalm 1:3 (NLT) - 3They are like trees planted along the riverbank, bearing fruit each season. Their leaves never wither, and they prosper in all they do.

Being homosexual, whether lesbian or gay, robs a human from being able to produce any offspring in the natural. How much more in the spiritual? There is no natural fruit produced from this union and no spiritual fruit produced for God's kingdom. In both places, the devil has robbed you from the possibility of multiplying. You have nothing to show for your life. Instead, you live a tormented existence of always fighting for a "right" to do something. This is not living; this is at best, surviving. According to John 10:10, God has called you to have life and to have it more abundantly.

The Hope

Is there hope for someone to regain their original identity if they have given themselves over to the rewiring of the mind for homosexuality? Yes, there is! There is hope because Jesus came and died to deliver man from the sinful nature. Homosexuality thrives in the sinful nature of mankind. However, Jesus' blood washes us from all sins and wickedness and He gives a clean, fresh start.

1 John 1:9 (NLT)- 9 But if we confess our sins to him, he is faithful and just to forgive us our sins and to cleanse us from all wickedness.

Titus 3:5-7 (AMP) - 5 He saved us, not because of any works of righteousness that we have done, but because of His own compassion and mercy, by the cleansing of the new birth (spiritual transformation, regeneration) and renewing by the Holy Spirit,

6 whom He poured out richly upon us through Jesus Christ our Savior,

7 so that we would be justified [made free of the guilt of sin] by His [compassionate, undeserved] grace, and that we would be [acknowledged as acceptable to Him and] made heirs of eternal life [actually experiencing it] according to our hope (His guarantee).

The devil cannot steal the hope that is found in Jesus; he can only steer you away from it with thoughts of offense against the God who created you. Don't give into the offense and lie that God made you different and that you're stuck and can never be changed. This is the problem to begin with, you were changed into what God didn't create,. God knows how to recreate you to be what He intended for you to be in the first place. Instead of dwelling on what the enemy says you are, start meditating about who God says you are.

Psalm 49:3 (KJV) - 3 My mouth shall speak of wisdom; and the meditation of my heart shall be of understanding.

The psalmist says out loud, with his own voice, what he plans to say with his mouth and what he wants his heart to think about. These are key components for you to start focusing on in order to regain the identity God created you to have. If you have abandoned yourself to the lifestyle of homosexuality, you can be rescued and restored into God's plan for your life once again.

Cry out to God for forgiveness and deliverance. Believe in your heart that Jesus is the Messiah and He is the only way to the Father. Receive Jesus as your Savior and Lord. Ask God to cleanse you with the blood of Jesus. When you do this, you will feel a weight lifted from you and will be a new creature in Christ Jesus.

2 Corinthians 5:17 (KJV) - 17 Therefore if any man be in Christ, he is a new creature: old things are passed away; behold, all things are become new.

The Bible shows us that all things become new when you come under the covering of Christ. Your mindset of who you think you are, verses who God created you to be, will be renewed. Your mannerisms will change, your life style will change, and your behavior will reflect your new nature.

Once you've become a new creation, ask God to fill you with all He has for you. Ask specifically to be filled the Holy Spirit and fire like they had on the day of Pentecost in Acts 2. Read it for yourself to see what God did for the believers in the upper room. The power of God in you will cause havoc for any evil spirit that tries to overtake you. You will cause the enemy to run scared for the rest of your life. You will never have to run from the enemy again. Now you will turn the tables on him. He will become *your* victim, not the other way around.

FIONA PYSZKA

CHAPTER 7

Position and Purpose Crisis

Your gender, age, or family position should not hinder your ability to follow God's purpose for your life. God knew that you would be a mother, father, son, or daughter when He assigned you your purpose. He took all of these positions of your life into account when He created you. Your position directly aides your purpose.

It is the enemy who comes in to tell you otherwise. This is why men and women find themselves bowing to the religious and cultural pressures to behave a certain way. When someone does not know the difference between what is allowed and what is ordained by God as a divine purpose, they will follow the wrong direction. They will either follow someone they admire and think is successful, or they will follow their own will and standard of what they think is right.

Position

The Bible has answers to help you know for sure what your role is on earth according to how God designed you to live and operate in His Kingdom. Once you become born again, you get the privilege of operating as an ambassador for the Kingdom of God on this earth. You get to benefit from God's divine order, setup and value He places on His creation. However, if you are not part of the Kingdom of God, you are subject to the systems of man that label you based on their thoughts of what you're allowed to do or are capable of doing. You are at the mercy of the system of the earth when you are not hooked up to the Kingdom of Heaven. It is your choice!

Many cultures today devalue women and children. They consider them to be property and not people. Before a girl has an opportunity to even speak her own name, she may already have been designated as the bride of a man much older than her. She is a bargaining chip for her family's financial future. This is not how God views women and children. This is not how Jesus treated them when He lived on the earth. Jesus scolded adults who dismissed children and He talked to women no one wanted as a friend.

A good example of this is found in the story recorded in John 4. The Samaritan woman was hated by all the women in her village. Her reputation was "husband-stealer." She was most likely manipulative and always had her way. In the natural, it would be easy to dismiss such a person, putting her in a category of a "loose woman." Yet, Jesus met her at her daily activity center, the well. He told her the story of her life and why she needed something that would last, instead of the quick fixes she had been accustomed to.

It is awesome to have a Savior that reaches out to us in our most awful state to rescue us from further destruction. God sees both men and women as repairable, restorable, and capable of changing their cities. The Samaritan woman became very influential in bringing her city to Jesus. Right away, after Jesus filled her with life-giving water, she produced a harvest of souls for Jesus to speak to. How awesome! Jesus did not stop her from sharing with the town because she was a woman. Rather, He empowered her to be a witness for Him. He gets the glory, not her gender.

In God's Kingdom the plan from the King is to have everyone be equal in His sight, whether man, woman or child. Everyone has the opportunity to access everything that Jesus paid for at the cross. Once a person receives Jesus as their Savior, they have direct access to God. They do not have to go through someone else to talk to God. They can now freely talk to and receive instructions from God. Equal access is granted to all Kingdom residents.

Galatians 3:28 (AMP) - 28 There is [now no distinction in regard to salvation] neither Jew nor Greek, there is neither slave nor free, there is neither male nor female; for you [who believe] are all one in Christ Jesus [no one can claim a spiritual superiority].

It is not God's will nor is it His plan for you to submit to someone else above His will or His plan for you. God in His Kingdom has perfect order and perfect protocol. Whatever He asks of you becomes your highest priority and you do not need any other person's approval or agreement to do what God has asked you to do. Simply obey God. For example, if someone is asking you to agree with them to not assemble with other Christians, then that is not from God. Here is what God's Word says that directly opposes that instruction.

Hebrews 10:25 (AMP) - 25 not forsaking our meeting together [as believers for worship and instruction], as is the habit of some, but encouraging one another; and all the more [faithfully] as you see the day [of Christ's return] approaching.

In the book of Acts, people of like precious faith met together daily and worshiped and praised God. They all did it according to Galatians 3:28, not caring what gender they were or what race, job, or position. Everyone worshiped together. As a matter of fact, they bonded so well and were in such unity that those with more possessions than others sold extra properties and material possessions they had and shared the profits with those who did not have enough.

Acts 2:44 (AMP) - 44 And all those who had believed [in Jesus as Savior] were together and had all things in common [considering their possessions to belong to the group as a whole].

This was not the developing of a cult, but the result of changed hearts, turned from selfishness to love. People were starting to think like God would. They started to look out for the welfare of others, rather than their own needs. Selfishness was at an all-time low once the gospel was introduced to the people.

The gospel of Jesus needs to be your obsession. When you throw your whole life into bringing the good news of what Jesus can do for people, you are on the right track to fulfilling your purpose, and you are certainly standing in the right role and position in the Kingdom of God. Jesus commissioned His disciples to multiply themselves. Whether they be man, woman or child, the commission was to make disciples all over the world. The same commission is given to you and me. We are to make disciples for the Kingdom of God. We are to all participate in this mandate. There is no sanction to stop men, women, or children from doing this. We see in Mark 16, Jesus told every disciple to go into all the world and preach the gospel to all creation. Jesus did not only direct this request to one gender or age group. He requested all hands on deck. Every believer of Jesus has the responsibility to follow this instruction to preach the gospel. He still wants this today. Will you do what He asked?

Mark 16:15 (AMP) - 15 And He said to them, "Go into all the world and preach the gospel to all creation.

A story comes to mind about how Jesus fed the five thousand. He was teaching all day and healing the sick. The evening came and the people were hungry. Before Jesus ended His session He wanted to feed them. The disciples were shocked at this and didn't know how they could make this happen. Then a little boy's lunch was discovered.

John 6:9 (AMP) - 9 "There is a little boy here who has five barley loaves and two fish; but what are these for so many people?"

Just like a little boy's lunch was used for God's Kingdom work, God wants to use what's in your hand for His kingdom also. Going into all the world to preach the gospel is for everyone to do: man, woman or child. Everyone is allowed to work in God's Kingdom, no one is excluded. No matter your gender, race, or position on earth, sharing the good news about what Jesus did for mankind is your job. Where you share it is also not a problem with God. You can share in a church, on the streets, one-on-one, or through any form of media. The goal is to share and not stop sharing. The whole world must hear the gospel and experience the power of

God. It is critical that we do this.

Purpose

God has specific reasons for each person being on earth. Your identity feeds and supports your purpose. For example, if God created you to be a musician in His Kingdom, then the cells in your body probably respond to musical sounds like nobody else can. You may hear a beat in your head for every word someone speaks. You probably see musical notes and songs no matter where you are. This identity of yours is in keeping with the purpose God has for you. To fine tune this purpose, find out specifically what people group or place He may have prepared for you to function in as a musician.

If you don't find out the when and where of your purpose, you may end up being rejected in places *you* decide to go instead of the places that Holy Spirit leads you to. This rejection can cause you to take on offense and get bitter at people. Once you are bitter at people, your tree will start producing sour fruit. You will become an offended brother or sister.

Proverbs 18:19 (AMP) – 19 A brother offended is harder to win over than a fortified city, And contentions [separating families] are like the bars of a castle.

You will declare yourself misunderstood and take up a defensive stance for the rest of your life. Every place you go from then on will always be with an attitude of defending yourself instead of presenting your gift. You will always be at war with people, fighting for a place to showcase your gift.

God's way, however, is that your gift should make room for you. In other words, when you go where the Spirit of God leads you, you are going to a place already prepared to receive you.

Proverbs 18:16 (AMP) - 16 A man's gift [given in love or courtesy] makes room for him and brings him before great men.

Your gift was created to be a weapon against the enemy, not against the people who are to be your audience. The people and places God has called you to will benefit from your gift and thus receive from your purpose. But, if you share your gifts with a bad attitude or a forceful gesture, you are turning a good opportunity into a war declaration.

Your gift and your purpose are not the same thing, but your gift is needed to help fulfill your purpose. For example, your gift may be to sing and play musical instruments; however, your purpose may be to create sounds of heaven on earth to allow people to worship God with all of their hearts. Do you see the difference? It's not just about your singing or playing of an instrument, but about the journey you are responsible to take people on. Maybe you are very gifted in accounting. Your gift is with understanding and analyzing numbers. However, this does not mean that your purpose in life is to be an accountant. Your purpose may be to help people solve number problems, whether it is through accounting, teaching math, or being a financial advisor. In these examples, you can see that your gift is just a tool given to you to help you fulfill your purpose for being on earth.

Why is it important to understand the difference between

your gift and your purpose? You may enjoy the talented singers and musicians of our day, and thought, "Wow, *if only I could sing or play an instrument like that.*" They may be talented, yet their music only touches you temporarily. It doesn't eradicate hopelessness or give you everlasting joy. Why? They may be using their gift (which God will not take from them, no matter if they choose God or not) but they are not fulfilling their purpose. You cannot fulfill your purpose if you are not a new creation in Christ living for the Kingdom of God. Their gift is singing and playing musical instruments, but their purpose may be to bring people into the presence of God through worshiping God. Instead, they have brought people into *their presence* to worship their gifts and talents, not the Creator who gave it to them.

Don't get me wrong, your *gift* may have saved mankind from a plague or invented technology that opened communication to save lives, but if you are not walking in the Kingdom of God, you cannot fulfill God's full *purpose* for your life.

God's purpose for your life is doing God's will. To do God's will you have to listen to God's voice. To hear God's voice you need to be led by Holy Spirit. God has sent us here so that we can live with him for eternity. If we are not born, we cannot dwell with Him. To be born, we have to come to earth. Earth is where God created His image. It wasn't in heaven, it was right here on earth. Jesus even had to come to earth to secure eternal life for us all. It could not be done from heaven: it had to be done from earth.

Genesis 1:26 (AMP) - 26 Then God said, "Let Us (Father, Son, Holy Spirit) make man in Our image, according to Our likeness [not physical, but a spiritual personality and moral likeness]; and let them have complete authority over the fish of the sea, the birds of the air, the cattle, and over the entire earth, and over everything that creeps and crawls on the earth."

John 3:16 (AMP) - 16 "For God so [greatly] loved and dearly prized the world, that He [even] gave His [One and] only begotten Son, so that whoever believes and trusts in Him [as Savior] shall not perish, but have eternal life.

A person will experience an identity crisis if they do not realize these two concepts: First, God created them to be fully submitted to Him directly without having to get permission from another person. Second, God has a specific purpose for them to fulfill on earth, using gifts, abilities, love and favor from God and man.

Without the combination of these qualities working together, it is almost impossible to fulfill your purpose. You may know your purpose, you may take steps towards the place you need to be to do God's purpose, but if the heart condition of love is not right, then the results of your purpose will be, at best, frustrating. When your heart condition is not operating by love, you can end up hurting people instead of helping them. You will get into doing things by rules and regulations instead of by the freedom that love brings.

Jesus knew, understood and walked in God's purpose every day. Jesus did not go somewhere that God was not ready for Him to be; He did not heal where God's healing power was rejected, and He did not do His own will even when it was nearly impossible to do God's.

John 11:6 (AMP) - 6 So [even] when He heard that Lazarus was sick, He stayed in the same place two more days.

John 5:19 (AMP) - 19 So Jesus answered them by saying, "I assure you and most solemnly say to you, the Son can do nothing of Himself [of His own accord], unless it is something He sees the Father doing; for whatever things the Father does, the Son [in His turn] also does in the same way.

Mark 14:36 (AMP) - 36 He was saying, " Abba, Father! All things are possible for You; take this cup [of judgment] away from Me; but not what I will, but what You will."

These verses show the life of Jesus as He used His gifts and abilities and fulfilled His purpose. The gifts and abilities Jesus operated in were fueled by the power of Holy Spirit. What are your gifts powered by? Whose power propels you forward into the gifts that God has put in you? The power that propels you will be the power that gets the glory.

God wants all of the glory from your life. He wants to be able to walk alongside you as you go through this thing called life. If you would like more information on discovering God's purpose for your life, check out my book, *The Purpose of You.*

Recognize who you have been created to be, and go after it with passion, vigor and tenacity. Fight where God asks you to fight, and walk away from where God asks you to leave. Don't hold on tight to earth's accolades; aim for God's approval. People who love you may have plans for you, but God's plans are greater, better and well-thought out. He's had eternity to think about you, so let His thoughts become part of your life. Let them become *your* reality.

CHAPTER 8

Depression Suppresses You

Depression has been given a lot of attention recently in the world. It has been labeled a disease and people who are "labeled" with it are expected to manage this for their lifetime. We must put in perspective the cruel joke the enemy plays on human lives with the trap of depression.

Let's examine its root and how it gets into someone's life. There is a story in the Bible that talks about a man named Job. Bible scholars and Christians alike seem to have differing views of what happened to "poor old" Job. It seems that God was punishing him for something, or some think that God was using him to teach mankind a lesson. Others debate that because he was so rich he had to be brought down to size. But what is the real truth? To find real truth, the Bible is the best source. We see in the Bible that Job says himself what has brought on his plight.

Job 3:25 (NLT) - 25 What I always feared has happened to me. What I dreaded has come true.

What Job had always feared and dreaded came upon him, suddenly, making him a byword. It is no mystery why Job went through what he did. It was a consequence of what he had entertained in his mind and home. Although Job was a righteous, God-fearing man, he was still responsible for whom he let in his house and for what lies he believed about himself, his children, and his possessions. Although God thought highly of his servant Job and was pleased with how much Job loved Him, God could not protect Job's property and family from the guest Job entertained in his heart and mind. Who was Job's guest? None other than the spirit of fear. Job allowed the spirit of fear to have its way in him.

The topic of fear is an extensive and exhausting one. As a matter of fact, I wrote an entire book on the subject called *You Can Be Fearless*. In it I explained that fear is a spirit, not just a feeling or a passing thing. It is a tangible spirit that can only be eradicated by a spiritual force: the Spirit of power, love and a sound mind.

2 Timothy 1:7 (AMP) - 7 For God did not give us a spirit of timidity or cowardice or fear, but [He has given us a spirit] of power and of love and of sound judgment and personal discipline [abilities that result in a calm, well-balanced mind and self-control].

Along with personal sickness and the loss of property and family, what else did Job experience by giving place to the spirit of fear?

Job 30:15-16 (NLT) - 15 I live in terror now. My honor has blown away in the wind, and my prosperity has vanished like a cloud.

16 "And now my life seeps away. Depression haunts my days.

Because Job invited fear as his guest, he experienced depression. Fear is the houseguest that lets depression in. Wherever you see depression, look for what the person is afraid of. Fear leaves seeds of destruction on its first visit, then it keeps sending friends like depression, oppression, and suicide to reap its harvest.

No more!

It's time to tell the spirit of fear to go from you. How do you do that? You simply use the tools that God gave you. Paul told Timothy to deal with fear by using the Spirit of power, love and a sound mind. Because God did not give us the spirit of fear, we do not have to be hospitable to it. You need to treat fear so rudely that it shudders at the thought of entering your presence. Fear should mark your name on a "do not call ever again" list. The spirit of fear should run at the sound of your voice or the hint of your shadow. It should scream to depression, oppression and suicide to "get out of the vicinity" because you're coming. That's the response fear should have to your presence, your name, and the sound of your voice. This is possible when you activate the Spirit of God to operate in your life. You activate this power by believing that God's Word will work for you and by taking action to do what the scripture says to do. If you don't stop believing His Word and don't stop putting it into action, the Word of God *will* work for you.

Spirit of Power, Love and a Sound Mind

We saw earlier in 2 Timothy 1:7 what type of spirit God has given us. If you want to stop the spirit of fear from defeating your life, then you need to activate, by faith, the Spirit that God has given you to deal with him. When the Spirit of power, love and a sound mind is activated in you, you will operate at a high level of faith in the areas the spirit of fear once attacked. When fear tries to slither its way in, you will stop it immediately with your supernatural tools.

For example, if you operate in the Spirit of Power, you will not stand by and just tap the enemy out of the way. You will electrify the situation with power. When you attack a problem caused by the enemy, supernatural power will be released to render fear's actions useless.

You will also operate at a level of love that neither offense, defensiveness, or foolishness can infiltrate. The Spirit of Love in you will eradicate selfish motives and hurt feelings towards others. In other words, the enemy will have no leverage against you of hatred or revenge in your heart. This alone renders the enemy paralyzed. There is no one he can whisper about in your ear, telling you they don't like you. That will garner a negative response from you. You will simply respond with, "That's fine, God's love through me is enough to cover their sin against me."

1 Peter 4:8 (NLT) - 8 Most important of all, continue to show deep love for each other, for love covers a multitude of sins.

Faith is activated when you speak God's words on a subject and believe those words above any other feelings, situation or tempting offers from the enemy. Thus, to operate by faith in the Spirit of a sound mind, you believe God's word about you having a sound mind, and it will render the enemy's words against you useless. Your mind will be fully secured and surrounded by the Word of God and will be able to detect and reject the lies of the enemy. This is where renewing the mind makes sense and works for you. You can daily renew your mind on things that have been wrongfully understood. You can renounce evil ways, ways that God's Word would never back up or support. Some examples are, plans to get revenge for who has wronged you, or thoughts of worrying about what you're going to do with a deficit in any area of life. You will stop entertaining anxious thoughts about the future of your children, or what they are involved in behind your back. All of these mind games will stop once you've activated faith in the Spirit of a sound mind. God has this for you and wants you to walk in it, but the only way to operate is to believe God gave you the Spirit of power, love and a sound mind.

This simply means that you believe God's Word concerning fear and it's antidote. You don't wonder how it works, you just agree that it will work. You agree that it will work for you, not just someone else.

King David went through a bout with depression, but he called on God to help him overcome. Here's what he said:

Psalm 143:4 (NLT) - 4 I am losing all hope; I am paralyzed with fear.

7 Come quickly, Lord, and answer me, for my depression deepens. Don't turn away from me, or I will die.

Listen to the desperate cry of a king as he deals with the vice of depression brought about by "fear". David had urgency for relief. That may be where you are today. Maybe you're at the end of your rope. Maybe you're losing hope and feeling hopeless. You may have lost the will to live or do anything meaningful. This is all evidence of the effects of the putrid spirit of fear that has left its residue in your life.

Clean that stench of failure from your life with the precious blood of Jesus and the mighty Spirit of God. The Spirit of power, love and a sound mind must be activated in you. Rise up from where you are. Submit to God, resist the devil and he will flee from you (see James 4:7).

The devil cannot dwell in or around a vessel that is submitted to God. He will flee, not just leave, but flee, running for his life. Your identity is too important to be hijacked by the spirit of fear. You are too important to the earth and God's plan for eternity to let the enemy come in and rob you of precious time and resources.

At the end of Job's bout with the enemy, God told Job to pray for his friends. This activated the spirit of power, love and a sound mind and God restored to Job double what he lost during the ordeal. This is proof that God is for you and not against you. He is always waiting to bless you, pour more upon you, and rescue you from distress. You have to believe it and walk it out in faith.

Job's prayer for his friends was his final act of detonating the spirit of fear. Before the ordeal all started, Job was hailed as a righteous man whom God admired.

Job 1:1 (AMP) - 1 There was a man in the land of Uz whose name was Job; and that man was blameless and upright, and one who feared God [with reverence] and abstained from and turned away from evil [because he honored God].

By the end of fear's time in Job's life, he went through a tongue-lashing from his friends and his own questioning of what God was doing to him. God wanted to reset Job's identity. He wanted Job to go back to being the righteous, God-fearing man he was when this started. God did this by asking Job to pray for the same people who accused him wrongfully, his friends. God asked Job to pray for those who blamed what happened to him on his behavior or lack of holiness, instead of recognizing that all he did was let the wrong guest stay in his house. That was all that Job did "wrong". He allowed fear to camp out in his house. Even when Job's wife asked him to curse God and die, Job wouldn't oblige. This is how God-fearing Job was.

You too may be quite the God-fearing person. Yet, you deal with depression on a regular basis. As a matter of fact, your whole life may have been plagued with episodes of depression that show up unannounced. I'm telling you today that the root of this fruit of depression is called fear. If you can learn how to have faith in God instead of giving attention to fear, you will defeat depression once and for all. It will never have to be a problem for you ever again.

You must get rid of depression in order to live a fulfilled life. Walking in your God-given identity requires it. You must be free from the camouflage of fear operating as "waiting" on the Lord before you make a decision. You must stop announcing how unqualified you are for what God is asking you to do. All of these excuses hinder God's work in your life and prepare living quarters for the spirit of fear to camp out with you. Evict fear and invite the Spirit of power, love and sound mind as a permanent resident in your home.

Take action today and watch how you will flourish in your life. Watch how quickly you will be breaking records and doing exploits for God.

Fear's motive is to take you down, but God's plan is to keep building you up. God wants to see you go from glory to glory.

Practical Actions To Take Now

Here are some practical ways that you can remove yourself from the pillars of depression that are holding you down.

1. Immediately contact someone to pray *for* you not *with* you. The reason is that you may be unable to agree with a prayer about your own life, so it's better for someone else to take matters to the Father, interceding on your behalf. Here is a list of things you should ask them to pray for concerning you:

   a. Ask God for His light to light up the darkness affecting you. - 2 Samuel 22:29

   b. God's cloud to cover you and His fire to light the darkness affecting you. - Psalm 105:39

   c. The Lord remove you from captivity, like in a dream, and fill your mouth with laughter. Psalm 126:1-2

   d. You will no longer live as a slave to depression: you live as an heir of Christ, walking in all the fullness of what you have inherited. - Galatians 4:7

2. Speak this declaration over your environment. Print

copies and place in locations around your home, office, vehicles and any other location you spend time.

a. I declare light into my environment, like God did in the beginning when He saw darkness and a void, empty waste. He declared light, and light shone in the darkness. *Genesis 1:3*

b. I declare that I am the righteousness of God in Christ Jesus, and no weapon formed against me shall prosper. *2 Corinthians 5:21; Isaiah 54:17*

c. I declare that I am well able to take the land that God has given me and no oppression from the enemy to steal God's gift from me will prosper. *Numbers 13:30*

d. I declare that I have angels right now working on my behalf to prevent me from dashing my foot against a stumbling block. I will have no debilitating obstacles in my way. *Psalm 91:11*

e. I declare that I am free, and I function with a clear mind to fulfill my destiny written before the foundations of the world. *1 Peter 5:8*

f. I declare that I am not a sleeping, slumbering fool. I am a wise, diligent person that achieves greatness for God's Kingdom. *Isaiah 5:27; Proverbs 4:23; Proverbs 12:24; Exodus 15:26*

g. I declare that I am the head and not the tail. I do

not agree with the lies of darkness, but I agree with the light of God's Word. *Deuteronomy 28:13*

h. I declare Jesus is my Lord. Jesus is my King. Jesus created me whole, and I am whole in Jesus' Name. *Matthew 9:22; Matthew 15:28*

i. I declare that I was created to sing to the Lord and praise God. I have rejoicing thoughts that please God. *Psalms 104:33-34*

3. Never be alone without sound around you. Your thoughts are the breeding ground for depression to maintain its hold and gain new ground in your life. Therefore, it is imperative that you never be alone without sound coming to you from external sources. A good habit to develop is to have music that will lift your spirit playing at all times. Watch comedy shows that will make you laugh. Listen to sermons, or listen to scriptures being read to music.

Depression is a bully and fights for all of your attention. Your attention to it only multiplies the ground it steals from your life. Therefore, give attention to things that will build you up and add to your life, instead of trying to just maintain your normal everyday routine. Choose to make the declarations listed here. It will create an atmosphere around you that is conducive to the Spirit of God moving. Just like the Spirit of God moved when He said "Light be!" in the beginning.

If you choose to build your life in spite of depression, depression will want to leave because it will no longer be your main focus. Depression hates to be shared with others. It wants all of your time. Keep this in mind as you leap to freedom. You have accepted another love, the word and work of God. Let this new love become your forever focus.

FIONA PYSZKA

CHAPTER 9

Reset Your Identity: Principle: Asking

So far, you have learned that there is a difference between your identity and your purpose. You have learned that the Word of God is a powerful tool to renew your mind and gain understanding. You also realized that there are things that mar your identity and block it from being expressed. You learned that the devil cannot just come and steal your identity; he needs your permission.

Now you're going to learn how to reset your identity. Resetting your identity means getting rid of anything that has blocked you from living in victory using your God-given identity. As you saw in earlier chapters, there are things that can hinder your identity from functioning optimally. Now you can proactively reset your life to function in the fullness of who God created you to be. Resetting your identity helps you to eradicate side effects of past trauma or mistakes in your life.

You may have encountered tragic experiences in life. Maybe you were badly abused and mistreated. You may be living in paralyzing fear. Depression may be your comfortable place, or maybe a mere lack of knowledge has kept you stagnant and frustrated. Not anymore. Now you will learn how to reset your identity with keys that will change your life forever.

You have to change your thinking by renewing your mind constantly on this information until it becomes the default action you take, no matter what happens or has happened to you. Let's take a look at some examples of people whose identity was reset using tools available in God's Word.

Jabez Asked God

Your first step to an identity reset is to use your mouth to ask. Who should you ask and what should you ask for? Well, let's take a look at a man named Jabez.

In 1 Chronicles we see a little excerpt of his life. Nothing extravagant, just that he got a name which identified him as "pain." We also see how easy it was for him to reset the label his name gave to him. Jabez asked God to reverse what was spoken to him from birth by his mother.

1 Chronicles 4:9-10 (NLT) –

9 There was a man named Jabez who was more honorable than any of his brothers. His mother named him Jabez because his birth had been so painful.

10 He was the one who prayed to the God of Israel, "Oh, that you would bless me and expand my territory! Please be with me in all that I do, and keep me from all trouble and pain!" And God granted him his request.

You may be trying to overcome negative words or labels spoken to you by people in your life. If that's what you've been doing your whole life, it's time to stop! Stop trying to get rid of their words; instead, start pursuing God with your own words.

Trying to undo what people say about you is a futile

endeavor, because it puts your focus on the voice of man instead of the plan of God. When you live life focusing on what you don't want to be, you end up setting those "do not's" as goals instead of targets that should be shot down. Your mind does not understand if a goal is negative or positive; it operates based on what you ask it to do. Your mind considers what you focus on the most to be what you want to accomplish. Your mind will then tell your brain to send signals to your body to start accomplishing the thoughts you have been focusing on the most. If you focus on what people think you are, your mind will receive these thoughts as an instruction from you and start rewiring your brain to become what they say.

For example, if you always believed that you were a great public speaker, but after a few speaking engagements people criticized your content and style. If you are not confident that public speaking is something you were created to do, you could now take the negative feedback and rewire your brain to believe you hate public speaking, convincing yourself that you should no longer be a public speaker.

By thinking this way you are subduing the true you and exalting the you that people think is your destiny. They created a route for your life that was not sanctioned by your Creator. They set you up for failure.

You may have been going around and around with non-stop movement, with the busyness of life, yet never really getting anywhere. It's time for no growth and slow growth to cease.

It is now time for you to rise up and shine. Shine as the person God created, the person He had in His mind, since before He said "Light, be!" on the earth.

When God formed this earth and all of its resources, He had you in mind. He knew that you would be on it and would need the things that He put here. He put everything you need to do what you have to do, right here on earth. He knew where He planned for you to live, to raise a family and to do work for Him. How can I make such a bold statement, you may wonder? Simple! Because it's what He did for Adam and Eve. He created a Garden of Eden for them. He settled them there, and gave them work to do. He even met with them right there. These actions by God were a model for how He expected the earth to respond to His people, those created in His image.

Your identity was established by God before your parents saw you in your first ultrasound. Before they ever heard your heartbeat, God had already determined your identity. The name your parents gave you is subject to change if you want it to. God is the source of making things change in your life. Ask Him today! Ask Him now. Pray to Him like Jabez did.

Jabez followed God's ways closely. He was the most honorable of all the children of his family. Yet, he was given a label that was unfit for his identity. So, Jabez appealed to the highest Judge in the universe, and upon his first appeal, he received favor. Jabez's life changed forever. His change was supernatural and quick.

How long have you been waiting for your life to reset? How

long have you been waiting for change to happen so you can be happier, more successful, or just "normal"?

Like Jabez did, just ask. The prayer he prayed may not have even taken him thirty seconds, but it gave a lifetime result. Take a moment now and ask like Jabez did, and God will reset your destiny to match His will for you.

Let's Pray - Father, I ask you to remove any labels placed on me from family, friends or people in authority. I agree with your destiny and plan for my life. I ask for a reset in any area that was given over to someone else, or taken away from me. I ask instead for You to bless me indeed. In Jesus' Name, Amen.

Ruth Asked Naomi

Ruth was another person that had her identity reset by asking God. The story of Ruth is fascinating and redemptive. She was a Moabite woman who was married to a Jewish man. After about ten years of marriage, he died. Only, he wasn't the only man in the family to die. Both her brother-in-law and father-in-law died during that same time. Ruth was a young widow. She was left with no men in her life. The women in her life were also mourning and contemplating their future. As a matter of fact, her mother-in-law Naomi's loss was so great that she changed her name to "Mara" meaning bitter.

Ruth 1:20 (NLT) - 20 "Don't call me Naomi," she responded. "Instead, call me Mara, for the Almighty has made life very bitter for me.

Ruth made a life-changing decision to go with her mother-in-law to a country she was unfamiliar with. She decided to relocate her life. By doing this she inadvertently reset her identity. Instead of being known as the widow of Kilion, she was now going to be known for something incredible.

Ruth 1:4-5(NLT) - 4 The two sons married Moabite women. One married a woman named Orpah, and the other a woman named Ruth. But about ten years later,

5 both Mahlon and Kilion died. This left Naomi alone, without her two sons or her husband.

Ruth's reset came as a result of her persistence of asking Naomi to take her to this new country. She was determined to make the change. She did not know at the time what a significant action she was taking, but she was ready to move on. She left her country and familiar surroundings to follow her bitter mother-in-law to a new land.

No matter what Naomi said to persuade her to stay in her comfort zone, she rejected those words, and kept asking. Little did she know that she was stepping right into God's future for her. Her real identity of bravery and persistence had come to light.

Just as Ruth persisted in asking Naomi to take her along, you must also be persistent in asking people for what you need from them. For example, if you need a job, ask the right people that can give you the job or help you network to find one. Don't let your past or present rejection stop you from asking.

Ruth's request not only reset her identity, but it allowed us to benefit from her life as well. Read her story in the Bible, in the book named after her. Then in the New Testament, we find that she was named in the lineage of Jesus, the Savior of the world. Ruth left her world to participate in the life of the One that would save the whole world. How awesome is that!

Matthew 1:5-6 (NLT) - 5 Salmon was the father of Boaz (whose mother was Rahab).Boaz was the father of Obed (whose mother was Ruth). Obed was the father of Jesse.

6 Jesse was the father of King David. David was the father of Solomon (whose mother was Bathsheba, the widow of Uriah).

Ruth's request changed the course of her life. She could have followed Naomi's advice, gone back to her country, and mourned all of the losses she had encountered. It seems that her sister-in-law, Orpah, did just that. We've never heard about Orpah again. But Ruth refused to be told "no" to a new life. She overturned Naomi's words with her own persistent asking. As a result she became the wife of a rich man named Boaz, a mother, and she restored joy back to Naomi.

God had designed Ruth to touch Boaz's field with her DNA. She was created to be part of his family. Her design was masterfully carved out by God to cause her to be attractive to him. The Bible tells us in Ruth 2 that Boaz noticed her working in the field. He inquired about her. I'm sure she was not the only woman working in the field; neither was she the only "pretty" young one. But, she was the only one with the correct identity for God's plan with Boaz. She was tagged from before the beginning of time to be in the lineage of Jesus.

Don't let the enemy's plan for your life be the period at the end of your sentence. Let God blot out the evil planned by the enemy and replace it with the plan that submits to His identity for you. Let Him be the deciding factor of when you stop and when you go. Keep His plans close to your heart, and attend daily to His instructions.

No Regrets

Don't live in regret and compromise your future for a cheap thrill of revenge. Leave the heavy lifting of these things to God and run your race in life without any weights on. Weights in life pertains to holding grudges, unforgiveness, revenge for wrongs done to you, or any other thing that captures your thoughts besides God's Word and plans for you. The book of Hebrews shows us this clearly.

Hebrews 12:1 (NLT) - 12 Therefore, since we are surrounded by such a huge crowd of witnesses to the life of faith, let us strip off every weight that slows us down, especially the sin that so easily trips us up. And let us run with endurance the race God has set before us.

God's plans for you are sound, and they will pass any test thrown at it. Just walk by faith, speak God's Word and expect life-changing results. Your identity can handle the pressure if the enemy tries to infiltrate. Don't let the enemy tell you the damage is irreparable. He's a liar. God is your Truth Giver. Ask for what you want to see happen in your life. Ask for the identity reset you need.

Practical Ways to Reset by Asking

Here are some practical ways in which you can apply the principle of asking to reset your identity.

1. Take a moment to consider who has your best interest at heart. You already know that God is your biggest fan. He wants the best for you in all areas of life. Therefore, He should be first on the list. Then consider what person could serve as a "Naomi" in your life - someone that is heading in the direction you need to go in order to live successfully in God's plan for you.

   a. Pray this prayer like Jabez did concerning your own life:

      i. Let's Pray - Father, I ask you to remove any labels placed on me from family, friends, or people in authority. I agree with your destiny and plan for my life. I ask for a reset in any area that was given over to someone else, or taken away from me. I ask instead for You to bless me indeed. In Jesus' Name, Amen.

   b. Ask the people on your list for what you would like to have from them and share a picture of your future vision. Asking is a terrifying thing for some people, however, think of it as a win-win. The person you're asking is probably looking for someone to help. Be their someone.

c. Maintain an attitude of asking God for repentance or help whenever you feel stuck in life. Feeling stuck could be a symptom of an identity issue or missing an instruction from God.

d. Utilize this verse regularly - *Matthew 7:7-8 (NLT)- 7 "Keep on asking, and you will receive what you ask for.* Keep on seeking, and you will find. Keep on knocking, and the door will be opened to you. 8 For everyone who asks, receives. Everyone who seeks, finds. And to everyone who knocks, the door will be opened.

God will always listen to what you have to say. He will respond to your asking faster than anyone else could. Ask Him and ask those who can help you for what you need today.

CHAPTER 10

Reset Your Identity: Principle: Taking Action

The phrase, "action speaks louder than words," may be familiar to you. Words without action is like living a lie. You plan to do many things, but rarely lift a finger to make it come to pass. When this practice keeps happening in your life, people will stop believing what you have to say. They will equate your words to an empty promise.

God takes action quickly, precisely, and frequently. Remember how quickly He kicked Satan out of heaven: so quick that when Satan fell, Jesus reported that he fell like lightning.

Luke 10:18 (AMPC) - 18 And He said to them, I saw Satan falling like a lightning [flash] from heaven.

When it comes to your identity God is not waiting on the right time and season to reset you to who He created you to be. He's waiting on you to take action. Your actions to do something about where you are and to stop believing what you know is not right about you are keys to being reset by God. These are keys to regaining your true identity in Christ. There's a story in the Bible about a man who kept waiting for someone else to help him heal. Let's take a look.

Waiting for Help

One day Jesus passed by the healing pool of Bethesda. He saw a man sitting there paralyzed. The man was just sitting there when Jesus asked him a question.

John 5:5-9 (NLT) - 5 One of the men lying there had been sick for thirty-eight years. 6 When Jesus saw him and knew he had been ill for a long time, he asked him, "Would you like to get well?"

7 "I can't, sir," the sick man said, "for I have no one to put me into the pool when the water bubbles up. Someone else always gets there ahead of me."

8 Jesus told him, "Stand up, pick up your mat, and walk!"

9 Instantly, the man was healed! He rolled up his sleeping mat and began walking! But this miracle happened on the Sabbath,

This man was paralyzed for thirty-eight years. Wow! This is how long this man had been living with a compromised identity. How do I know this? Well, sickness is not an identity that God created anyone to have. This man's identity was that he was a sick man, lying around for thirty-eight years. Sickness is not God's will, it will never be an identity that God puts as part of your life.

Besides, Jesus would never undo something that the Father did. We see here that Jesus asked the man if he wanted to get well. Jesus would not have asked the man to change from his current state if God was not in agreement. Whatever God is in agreement with is His will.

The answer this man gave Jesus was similar to what people say today. This man was expressing that he did not get healed as yet because he had no one to put him in the pool. He also pointed out that someone else got there before he could maneuver himself to the pool.

Does this sound familiar? "Well, I can't do what God wants me to do." "Someone already got the job before I could apply." Or, "I don't have enough education." Moses used this same type of excuse, telling God that he was a stutterer. These are all lame excuses that block the manifestation of your true identity. Whatever excuse you use to say "No" to God becomes a wall between you and your destiny. God holds your destiny. A "No" to Him keeps you in the same place, never moving forward. The place you're in now could have been a place of excellence at one time. However, if you keep staying there against God's will, it will become your place of failure.

The good news is that even though this man at the pool of Bethesda had excuses, Jesus still offered him healing. He accepted Jesus' healing and got healed immediately. Now that this man was healed, he had the ability to do what God created him to do. For sure we know that God did not create him to be sick for the rest of his life. God created him to take action for His Kingdom. Wasting away at the pool of Bethesda was not God's will for his life.

Abraham Took Action

The Bible calls Abraham the father of faith. He is a role model of faith for Christianity today. But did you know that none of this would be possible if he had stayed where his daddy, Terah, lived?

In Genesis 11 we see that Terah started on a journey to go to the land of Canaan, but he never got to his destination. Instead, he camped in Haran, named after his oldest son who died. He set up camp in a place of mourning and never left. The Bible shows that he died in Haran. Terah died at the place of mourning. He was paralyzed from moving forward from the death of his son. Leaving the place that was named after his loss was too hard for him to do, so it prevented him from taking action to move forward. God waited on him, but he did nothing to move on. So God visited His son, Abram, to dislodge him from his father's past and follow the direction God had predesigned for Terah's family.

In Genesis 12 we see that God tells Abram (his name was later changed to Abraham) to go to a place that He would show him. Abram's instructions were to get up and take action. His action would show his obedience.

Genesis 12:1-4 (NLT) - 1 The Lord had said to Abram, "Leave your native country, your relatives, and your father's family, and go to the land that I will show you.

2 I will make you into a great nation. I will bless you and make you famous, and you will be a blessing to others.

3 I will bless those who bless you and curse those who treat you with contempt. All the families on earth will be blessed through you."

4 So Abram departed as the Lord had instructed, and Lot went with him. Abram was seventy-five years old when he left Haran.

God found Abram living in the place of death his dad had set up for the family. What a lineage that would have been. Certainly we would have never heard of Abram had he not accepted God's beckoning. God had preordained Abram to be the father of faith, but he still had to participate in the plan.

If you read the amazing life of this father of faith, you will see that whatever God asked him to do, he was eager to do. The only mistake it seems he made in his life, was to not walk and take possession of all the land God had ordained for him and his posterity to possess. Abram's journey started at the age of seventy-five. He was told that he would be made a great nation. All the while, Abram was well aware that he had a barren wife. Yet, Abram took action and he moved towards God's vision for him, even though the vision included having children and grand, grand, grand, grand, children.

We see that God used Abram mightily. He changed Abram's name to Abraham and Sarai's name to Sarah. The name change of these two agents of God was an expression of how *God* saw them verses how their *family* saw them. Abraham's name change took him from being "exalted father" to "father of many nations." Sarah's name took her from "my princess" to "Princess." Sarah's new name reflected the influence she would have over nations instead of only her household. The name change gave them a better identification of who God created them to be. Their new names removed the limitation from only benefitting *their* lifetime to benefiting generations to come, including today's generation.

Genesis 17:3-5 (AMP) - 3 Then Abram fell on his face [in worship], and God spoke with him, saying,

4 "As for Me, behold, My covenant is with you, And [as a result] you shall be the father of many nations.

5 "No longer shall your name be Abram (exalted father), But your name shall be Abraham (father of a multitude); For I will make you the father of many nations.

Genesis 17:15 (AMP) - 15 Then God said to Abraham, "As for Sarai your wife, you shall not call her name Sarai (my princess), but her name will be Sarah (Princess).

God was changing Abraham's past before his very eyes. Abraham's name now announced his destiny wherever he went. Another adjustment that God had to do in Abraham's life was to remove people that were a hindrance to God's will for his life. God had to relocate Lot.

Lot, his nephew who came with him, represented the past. He was the son of Haran. He represented the dead brother. But then God showed up and changed a family, marking them for His formation of a chosen people.

As soon as Abraham sent Lot to his own location, God showed Abraham what He had planned to give him.

Genesis 13:14-17 (NLT) - 14 After Lot had gone, the Lord said to Abram, "Look as far as you can see in every direction—north and south, east and west.

15 I am giving all this land, as far as you can see, to you and your descendants as a permanent possession.

16 And I will give you so many descendants that, like the dust of the earth, they cannot be counted!

17 Go and walk through the land in every direction, for I am giving it to you."

Abraham's action to follow God's instructions not only got him out of a past of death, but into a future of life. Abraham's lineage became the line for Jesus' birth. Abraham took action for his own life even in the face of impossible situations.

Gideon, The Warrior

Judges chapters 6 and 7 is the story of God's people the Israelites moving from being afraid of their enemies, the Midianites, to triumphing over them in unprecedented fashion.

Gideon is seen while hiding in a winepress threshing wheat. Because of the oppression of the Midianites, the Israelites had to hide their harvest to keep it from being stolen. The oppression of this enemy was so bad, that as soon as it was time for the Israelites to harvest their crops, the innumerable army of the Midanites would come in and steal all of it. What a frustrating way to live.

This was the day-to-day struggle of the Israelites. It would be as if a large crowd of people would stand outside your house every time you got paid, taking all of your money before you even went inside. In this type of situation, the only way you could keep any money would be by doing side jobs and hiding the money where no one could find it.

This is the same situation the Israelites lived in every harvest season. They could not overcome the enemy in their own strength. Even though you may be hiding from the enemy, God knows where to find you and He knows how to help you. The psalmist said it best.

Psalm 139:7-8 (NLT) - 7 I can never escape from your Spirit! I can never get away from your presence!

8 If I go up to heaven, you are there; if I go down to the grave, you are there.

9 If I ride the wings of the morning, if I dwell by the farthest oceans,

10 even there your hand will guide me, and your strength will support me.

11 I could ask the darkness to hide me and the light around me to become night—

12 but even in darkness I cannot hide from you. To you the night shines as bright as day. Darkness and light are the same to you.

It is in this condition of hiding and fearfulness that God finds Gideon and pulls him from behind the scenes to the forefront of God's planned victory. Before Gideon was born, God had him picked as the one who would lead God's army into battle against this enemy. So, it didn't matter how big the enemy's army had become, God's records indicated a win for His people, and a win is what was about to take place.

In order for this victory to happen on earth as it was recorded in heaven, Gideon needed to take action. God came and spoke with Gideon, giving him specific instructions.

Judges 6:12 (NLT) - 12 The angel of the Lord appeared to him and said, "Mighty hero, the Lord is with you!"

14 Then the Lord turned to him and said, "Go with the strength you have, and rescue Israel from the Midianites. I am sending you!"

When God says, "I am sending you!" you don't have to fear

what will happen. Once God has sent you, victory is a guarantee. God's action in a situation will always result in victory for those He has sent. This is why you do not want to be God's enemy, because whoever God sends to fight against you on His behalf will win. Satan thought he could win against God. He thought he knew how heaven operated: after all, he was a high ranking official. But what Satan forgot, and still doesn't seem to remember today, is that God can never lose, *ever*.

If you would realize that the battle strategies we see on earth have already been preplanned and written in heaven, then when it's time to fight, you will ask God which plan He has for you to use. You use it at His command and, *bam*, a win. A win for you is a win for God's kingdom. If you disobey God's instructions, you will lose the fight because you're not operating according to God's plan. However, you have until the fight is over to get the plan right. So don't beat yourself up if you've made a mistake along the way. Stop, reset, and keep moving.

If you choose to remain where you are because of fear, you will lose the fight. Being paralyzed by fear shows that you choose to take no action. If you could just develop your ear to hear God's voice, to follow it unashamedly and fearlessly, you will never lose a battle in life. Gideon accepted God's instruction and took action.

Because we have Holy Spirit living in us today, we do not have to test God. We simply test the spirit. We determine whether or not something is of God by listening to the Spirit of God in us. In Gideon's days, the Spirit of God did not dwell in people, so they would cast lots or do fleeces. We don't have to do that today; instead, we have Holy Spirit living in us. He knows all things and He is our leader and guide. God has set up a system in us to detect accurately when the enemy is asking us to do something or when He is asking us to do something. This system is the voice of God.

Practice following the voice of God in your life instead of your feelings on a matter. Don't look to your expertise in order to say "yes" to God. Look to God's instructions. If it's Him asking, say "yes" without hesitation. If it's the enemy, even if you can do it, always say "no." That's what Jesus did. Jesus did not turn the stones into bread, jump off a cliff, or bow to the enemy, even though He was capable of doing all those things. Instead, He answered the enemy with a "no" by sharing scripture that backed up His answers (see Matthew 4).

Examine The Motive of Your Heart

Your identity was created for you personally by God. He alone planned every detail of your uniqueness. He did not delegate this responsibility to His angels, or anyone else. He took care of your design Himself. We see this in Genesis when God called Jesus and the Holy Spirit to make man in Our own image.

Genesis 1:26 (AMP) - 26 Then God said, "Let Us (Father, Son, Holy Spirit) make man in Our image, according to Our likeness [not physical, but a spiritual personality and moral likeness]; and let them have complete authority over the fish of the sea, the birds of the air, the cattle, and over the entire earth, and over everything that creeps and crawls on the earth."

His motive for being the personal designer of your identity is love. He loves you to the last detail of which you were created. God loves you beyond words or measure. There is no system, dimension, or frame of reference on this earth that could describe how much God loves you.

Psalm 36:5 (NLT) -5 Your unfailing love, O Lord, is as vast as the heavens; your faithfulness reaches beyond the clouds.

1 John 4:10 (NLT) - 10 This is real love—not that we loved God, but that he loved us and sent his Son as a sacrifice to take away our sins.

Your identity was sealed with God's love, so it responds to the operation of God's love in your life. There is something else on earth that cannot operate without love; faith. For this reason a life filled with love should be a major priority in your life. You should live everyday to firstly love God, then to love your neighbor as yourself. This motive of living by love will give you freedom in every area of life. It will cause you to be the envy of those who despise you and it will be the mark for which you are known in the spirit realm.

Galatians 5:6 (NLT) - 6 For when we place our faith in Christ Jesus, there is no benefit in being circumcised or being uncircumcised. What is important is faith expressing itself in love.

Jesus summed up the Ten Commandments into two commandments.

Matthew 22:36-40 (NLT) - 36 "Teacher, which is the most important commandment in the law of Moses?"

37 Jesus replied, "'You must love the Lord your God with all your heart, all your soul, and all your mind.'

38 This is the first and greatest commandment.

39 A second is equally important: 'Love your neighbor as yourself.'

40 The entire law and all the demands of the prophets are based on these two commandments."

Jesus answered questions from His critics by sharing powerful truths. He announced that everything that the law and the prophets demanded hangs on these two new commandments to love. We are to love God, love ourselves and love our neighbors.

If you don't love God, then there is no point in trying to love yourself or even your neighbor. Even if you think you love yourself or your neighbor, your love will lack the God-factor of love. Your love without God's love in you is simply selfishness and not admiration for God's version of you.

Let's examine more of this type of unselfish love in the next chapter. In the meantime, consider this question: do you truly love yourself for who God made you to be, or because of what you've accomplished? The biggest action you can take for your identity reset is to always walk in love.

CHAPTER 11

God's Love And Man's Love

Love is a powerful source that originates from God. Without God there can be no love, because God is love.

1 John 4:8 (NLT) - 8 But anyone who does not love does not know God, for God is love.

You cannot state that you love yet still deny God. It is impossible to have pure and true love and not know God. God is the source of love, so He has to operate through you in order for you to walk in love.

Walking in love is a sore subject for many people. I personally believe it is difficult because we forget that love is not a personal quality we possess, but a spiritual power we pull from. The Bible shows us that the fruit of the Spirit is love (see Galatians 5:22).

The works of the flesh do not carry the same value as the fruit of the Spirit. You must understand the difference between the two and stop trying to turn your flesh into pious spiritual vessels. Your flesh man needs to be put down daily. You need to put your desire for personal control under the total control of Holy Spirit, our gift from God.

Romans 8:12-14 (NLT) - 12 Therefore, dear brothers and sisters, you have no obligation to do what your sinful nature urges you to do.

13 For if you live by its dictates, you will die. But if through the power of the Spirit you put to death the deeds of your sinful nature, you will live.

14 For all who are led by the Spirit of God are children of God.

Your first level of identity needs to be with God. Identify as being a child of God. Once that is taken care of, you then identify as being a person that lives according to the Spirit of God and not your fleshly desires.

Your flesh has no recognition of the things of God, only your spirit man does. It is your spirit man that can determine whether God is speaking to you or the devil is giving you an instruction. The reason it's sometimes difficult to know if the devil is behind an instruction, is because he uses people that are part of your life, especially someone who loves you. We see an example of this after Peter announced the big revelation that he knew that Jesus is Lord. Of all the disciples there, Peter was the only one who got this revelation from the Spirit of God. However, in the next conversation, we see Jesus rebuking him as Satan. *Wow!* What happened?

The Trap of Avoiding Hurt

Let's take a look at the story of Peter's revelation of Jesus as Messiah.

Matthew 16:15-16 (NLT) - 15 Then he asked them, "But who do you say I am?"

16 Simon Peter answered, "You are the Messiah, the Son of the living God."

In this passage we see Jesus sharing with the disciples about His final act as Messiah before leaving earth. He was sharing this with them because they were His disciples. This was information that they could handle.

Matthew 16:21-23 (NLT) - 21 From then on Jesus began to tell his disciples plainly that it was necessary for him to go to Jerusalem, and that he would suffer many terrible things at the hands of the elders, the leading priests, and the teachers of religious law. He would be killed, but on the third day he would be raised from the dead.

22 But Peter took him aside and began to reprimand him for saying such things. "Heaven forbid, Lord," he said. "This will never happen to you!"

23 Jesus turned to Peter and said, "Get away from me, Satan! You are a dangerous trap to me. You are seeing things merely from a human point of view, not from God's."

Whooa! Jesus rebuked Peter as if He was rebuking Satan. His rebuke came because Peter was responding to Jesus' purpose with his human feelings, not with faith. Peter did not want Jesus to suffer pain or die, because he loved Him and saw himself as Jesus' ministry partner. Peter's fear of Jesus' future caused him to reprimand Jesus and thought Jesus was just speaking negatively about His future. When in fact it was Peter who was in error for walking in fear of what could happen to Jesus if He followed God's will. Have you ever done that to someone, or had someone do it to you?

Jesus knew His identity. He knew why He was sent to earth and what He was supposed to do. Jesus' description of the events that were about to unfold was not in torment or fear, but with expectation for a joyful end. Jesus was not asking permission; He was stating His mission. Jesus knew He was wired to accept and follow through with this request from God. Jesus was ready to do it.

But Peter was far from ready for Jesus to step out in faith and fulfill His destiny. Peter's flesh was having a meltdown. Peter's reaction was not just about what he didn't want Jesus to suffer, but about what would happen to him if the ministry he was now part of came to an end. He didn't know what would happen to all the people Jesus was healing and raising from the dead. Who would cast out all those demons? Peter's business plans for Jesus' ministry were fading before his very eyes.

These are the types of questions and responses you have when you see your life through the flesh instead of the Spirit of God. Worrying to keep things as they are becomes a priority in the mind. When your mind starts worrying, fear is activated to come and comfort you. Fear doesn't need your verbal request to be activated, it just needs you to take action based on your worry. What bothers your mind will result in the actions you take in your life. Your destruction and complete annihilation is the goal of fear in your life. You activate fear every time you worry about something.

Jesus knew this about fear. Hence the reason He strongly rebuked Peter. Jesus did not rebuke Peter simply because he was going against the plans Jesus had laid out. Jesus rebuked Him because the "counsel" he was giving Him was laced with worry and fear.

You may have well-meaning people in your life who want to

"help" you succeed, but they end up holding you back with their fear and worry. Taking steps of faith is foreign to them. All they know is that if you take too big a risk, you will get hurt. They just don't want you to be hurt.

So, what if you follow God's instructions and get hurt? Do you believe that God could bind up the broken hearted as mentioned in Psalm 147 and Isaiah 61? Following God's plan for your life is not a hurt-free zone, it is a winning zone. If you want to win battles every time and never get hurt, you're in the wrong line of spiritual activity. The truth is you may get hurt, no matter whose side you're fighting on. Whether you're fighting for God or against Him, you could get hurt. The difference is, if you're fighting *for* God you will win, if you're fighting *against* God you will lose.

Losing is what happens over and over again to someone who belongs to the kingdom of darkness. Just when they think they're winning, they experience a great, big loss.

Here's the moral of the story: you're going to encounter battles in life. I suggest you fight on the side that will always win and plan to stay on this winning side for life. You get on the winning side based on what you believe and by following the voice of Holy Spirit. Doubt will put you on the enemy's frequency of losing, but faith will keep you on God's frequency of winning.

At this statement you may be saying, "But I've been involved in fights and have lost. I've quoted the Word of God and prayed and still did not win, how can that be?" I think everyone has been there at some time. Let's examine what could be some possibilities.

Maybe you think the fight is over, but it's not -- so you stop fighting. If you discover that's your situation, keep attacking the enemy with the Word of God and your faith until the win comes. It could also be that you stepped out of God's battle plan of faith, and started using natural weapons like logic and emotions to fight. If this is the case, then learn from this mistake and take on future fights wearing your armor and using your weapons of spiritual warfare. Don't go to battle against the enemy with your logic or emotions. You will lose. He's been around a lot longer than you, and he knows how to play the war game you're trying to play with him. He knows *he* will lose if you use the Word of God against him. But, decade after decade, year after year, he waits and hopes for the person that will fall for his trap of doubt and fear. This is the person he can win against and secure a victory. Satan has never won a fight against God. So, use God's tools against him. Use the tools that have never lost to Satan.

2 Corinthians 10: (KJV) - 4 (For the weapons of our warfare are not carnal, but mighty through God to the pulling down of strong holds;)

One of the greatest weapons in God's kingdom is love. No battle is won without the ingredient of love slathered in every phase of the fight. You have to love God in order for His weapons to work in your hand. If your love for God is nonexistent or cold, then your battles will all be lost. Why? Because God's weapons and tools are activated by and operate by love.

Galatians 5:6 (NLT) - 6 For when we place our faith in Christ Jesus, there is no benefit in being circumcised or being uncircumcised. What is important is faith expressing itself in love.

In Galatians 5:6 we see that there is no benefit on how holy we look or behave. What is important instead is how our faith is expressed in love. Another translation says that "faith works by love." If you get into a battle and you are operating in the rituals you keep to show your Christianity but leave out love, you will lose. Love is the most important ingredient for your success.

Your love for God and love for your neighbor may be nonexistent, but you may not even realize it. It may have run cold. In the book of Revelation, one of the charges that God had against the church in Ephesus was their love running cold towards Him.

Revelation 2:1-6 (NLT) - 1- "Write this letter to the angel of the church in Ephesus. This is the message from the one who holds the seven stars in his right hand, the one who walks among the seven gold lampstands:

2 "I know all the things you do. I have seen your hard work and your patient endurance. I know you don't tolerate evil people. You have examined the claims of those who say they are apostles but are not. You have discovered they are liars. 3 You have patiently suffered for me without quitting.

4 "But I have this complaint against you. You don't love me or each other as you did at first!

5 Look how far you have fallen! Turn back to me and do the works you did at first. If you don't repent, I will come and remove your lampstand from its place among the churches.

6 But this is in your favor: You hate the evil deeds of the Nicolaitans, just as I do.

This verse shows a church that had honored God in many ways, yet He had one complaint against them. He charged them with not loving Him or each other, as they first did. This is *huge*! It's like the conversation some husbands and wives have after they've been married for a while and the wife or husband says, "You don't love me anymore." The other spouse may reply, "But of course I do. I told you I loved you the day we got married." Over the years, they took things for granted and gradually stopped saying, "I love you" and expressing love in a tangible way.

This is the same way some people have treated God. Still, year after year, they complain about having unresolved problems that God has not helped them fix. In Revelation 2, you see that God saw all the "good works" that this church was doing. He even saw that they hated the things He hated, but they did not love Him or each other anymore. Wow!

So how exactly are you to love God and love each other? What does God expect from you? He said in His Word exactly what you should do if you loved Him or loved your neighbor.

John 13:35 (AMP) - 35 By this everyone will know that you are My disciples, if you have love and unselfish concern for one another."

Romans 13:10 (AMP) - 10 Love does no wrong to a neighbor [it never hurts anyone]. Therefore [unselfish] love is the fulfillment of the Law.

John 21:17 (KJV) - 17 He saith unto him the third time, Simon, son of Jonas, lovest thou me? Peter was grieved because he said unto him the third time, Lovest thou me? And he said unto him, Lord, thou knowest all things; thou knowest that I love thee. Jesus saith unto him, Feed my sheep.

John 14:15 (NLT) - 15 "If you love me, obey my commandments.

In these verses the Bible lists the actions that God looks for to see and feel if you love Him. He also shows you what loving your neighbors should encompass. It is important to understand this concept because without loving God properly or your neighbor as you love yourself, you can hinder your true identity from working properly. You are setting yourself up for a malfunction in accessing what God has prepared for you.

Any malfunction in your armor is an opening for the enemy to attack. When living a successful life, you want to have all bases covered. You want to be protected on every side. God has prepared a way for you to experience this type of elite protection. He has established angels to protect you, and the Bible shows how He put a hedge of protection about you.

Job 1:10 (AMP) - 10 Have You not put a hedge [of protection] around him and his house and all that he has, on every side? You have blessed the work of his hands [and conferred prosperity and happiness upon him], and his possessions have increased in the land.

This hedge of protection is compromised when fear is present. Love keeps your hedge of protection intact. Fear and love cannot exist in the same place because fear is cast out by perfect love.

1 John 4:18 (AMP) - 18 There is no fear in love [dread does not exist]. But perfect (complete, full-grown) love drives out fear, because fear involves [the expectation of divine] punishment, so the one who is afraid [of God's judgment] is not perfected in love [has not grown into a sufficient understanding of God's love].

As you can see, love is a vital ingredient to waging a winning war against the enemy. Without love, you cannot win a battle. Why? Because without love your faith cannot work and fear gets access, which compromises your armor for warfare. The armor of God is highly dependent on the shield of faith (see Ephesians 6:16). If the shield of faith is not present the fiery darts of the devil will hit you, causing pain, making life hot and uncomfortable. Well, the shield of faith needs love to operate because as we learned earlier, faith works by love.

Your love walk must be guarded with all diligence. You guard it by not harboring thoughts of unforgiveness, revenge or false expectations of people. These are all distractions to fulfilling God's call on your life. Your identity does not provide you with storage facilities to store away your unforgiveness. It opens doors to love, joy, peace, longsuffering and the rest of the fruit of the Spirit (see Galatians 5:22).

To fix any identity issue you may have lingering in your life, you must fix your love walk -- the walk you have with God and the walk you have with man. All of it matters. How you love yourself matters greatly. If you can't love yourself, it's difficult to love your neighbor properly because you're supposed to love your neighbor as yourself.

Without a proper love walk, fear has free access to your life. Why? You will always be afraid of what people or God think about you. You will never give people or God the benefit of the doubt that they love you.

Fear brings with it torment. Torment is not a residue of love; it is a presence of fear. You must fix your love walk every time you feel that it is even slightly off.

Symptoms of a Lagging Love Walk

You may have a weak love walk with God if you find yourself unable to express your love to God, blaming God for something that went wrong in your life, or thinking that God is out to get you because you did something wrong. All of these thoughts about God and how He feels about you are wrong and will hinder your ability to love God or receive love from God.

It is a fact that we could never deserve God's love. After all we were all sinners, but thanks be to God for His redemption that has put us back in right standing with Him. God knows that we don't deserve His love, yet He chooses to give it to us freely as a gift. He does this because He is love and He loves. Our part is to receive God's love and not to reject it.

Rejection of God's love is a sure way to allow access to the enemy to treat you harshly, proving to you that you deserve to feel pain or be punished for the "bad" person you are. In God's eyes, He sees love as a remedy for the consequences of sin that Satan entices you with. So if you've missed the mark and sinned, God's love will still work for you, it just has to be received. A verse that just about everyone can recite from memory shows us this profound truth.

John 3:16 (AMP) - 16 "For God so [greatly] loved and dearly prized the world, that He [even] gave His [One and] only begotten Son, so that whoever believes and trusts in Him [as Savior] shall not perish, but have eternal life.

Before you could decide if you wanted to love God, He loved you. He loved you so much that He sent His best gift to earth just for you. He did not skimp on His gift, but He freely gave His only begotten Son for you to have the opportunity to receive eternal life.

Jesus came on the scene to remove mankind from the curse of eternal death, to eternal life. Adam and Eve lost eternal life for mankind, but because God loves man, He prepared a way for reconciliation. His way was prepared because of His love.

The enemy of your life wants to give you evidence against God and people in your life to hinder your love walk with them. Don't fall for his trap. Step over him and run to the arms of your loving Father. Run with fervency and determination the race of your life, forgiving in the next breath any wrongs that are levied against you. Don't leave time between a wrong done to you and your forgiveness of the person. The lag time between the offence and your forgiveness is space for the enemy to bombard your mind with lies. He will create scenarios in your mind that make the offence against you seem greater than it really was. When you believe a lie, the truth becomes distasteful to you. You must remember the enemy is the father of lies.

John 8:44 (NLT) - 44 For you are the children of your father the devil, and you love to do the evil things he does. He was a murderer from the beginning. He has always hated the truth, because there is no truth in him. When he lies, it is consistent with his character; for he is a liar and the father of lies.

Every lie you believe about God or your neighbor comes

from the father of lies. It did not come as a message from God, but was a dart of the enemy. Don't believe lies anymore about you or your neighbor. Choose to believe the truth of God's Word. Believe His truths especially written about you before the foundations of the world.

He knows you inside and out and chooses to love you. Don't push away His love, receive it. Open every part of you to receive it. Don't hesitate another moment. Do it now.

Pray this prayer now:

Father, I agree with your plan for my life. I agree with John 3:16 and how you sent Jesus for me. I accept and receive Your love for me. Thank you for loving me. I love you too Father and ask you to forgive me for doubting any of Your love towards me. I believe that your love was shed abroad in my heart (see Romans 5:5). In Jesus' Name. Amen!

FIONA PYSZKA

CHAPTER 12

You Have Been God Approved To Be Here

In the beginning of this book we discussed how God made you and approved of you. His creation of you was a direct result of the big plan He had in mind when He created the world. You are part of God's master plan for now and the ages to come.

Ephesians 2:7 (AMP) - 7 [and He did this] so that in the ages to come He might [clearly] show the immeasurable and unsurpassed riches of His grace in [His] kindness toward us in Christ Jesus [by providing for our redemption].

You're not a bother, neither are you a nobody to God. Actually, if you are born again, God considers you part of His royal family and priesthood.

1 Peter 2:9 (NLT) - 9 But you are not like that, for you are a chosen people. You are royal priests, a holy nation, God's very own possession. As a result, you can show others the goodness of God, for he called you out of the darkness into his wonderful light.

God made you for such a time as this. You are needed on this earth to function at full capacity. Fulfilling all of your assignments written before the foundations of the world is important to God and it should be important to you also.

No More Self Inflicted Pain

Stop undermining your position in God's Kingdom. Refrain from demeaning yourself anymore. Don't agree with the enemy's assessment of you. Remove the labels that people painted on you from birth. The blood of Jesus is powerful enough to wash away every stain, mark, or excuse you can think of to call yourself unworthy. God has made you worthy to work on His behalf and represent His Kingdom on earth.

Acts 5:41(AMP) - 41 So they left the Council, rejoicing that they had been considered worthy [dignified by indignity] to suffer shame for [the sake of] His name.

When you are convinced that God wants you here on earth to do His work, you will not be easily encumbered by the words of men to stop you. You will hold your ground because you know you belong here.

Fulfilling God's Plan

What hinders you from walking unashamedly into what God has asked you to do? Do you think of your hurtful past, your inabilities, or is it your desire for your own will? It is important to answer these questions in order to live a fulfilling, joyful life. If you stay hindered, you will live a stagnant life that will cause harm to you and those around you.

Rejecting God's assignment puts you in the path of the enemy's attack. It leaves you with a void in your life that causes you to feel that something is missing. When you feel empty, you keep searching for something, anything, that could fill the void. At this point, the enemy comes in to be your void-filling agent. He comes to give you ideas and suggestions of what you can do to fill the void. He will even offer "opportunities of a lifetime" to lure you further away from God's plan, making the void bigger and deeper. Whereas, God already had a plan to fill your void. God did not design you to have a void that remains, He designed you to have place in your heart to always receive His instructions. God's assignments were designed to fill open places in your life. When you say "no" to the instructions a void will remain.

Rejecting God's plans may be more common than you realize. This does not eject you from heaven; however, it causes your life here to be less than God planned for you.

Jeremiah 2:13 (NLT) - 13 "For my people have done two evil things: They have abandoned me— the fountain of living water. And they have dug for themselves cracked cisterns that can hold no water at all!

In Jeremiah, God talks about two evils that His people have done against Him. He was rejected and replaced with a container full of holes. In other words, people have rejected living water that needs no container because it flows directly from the Throne of God. They rejected this living water for an earthly pot that stays empty because no amount of water poured into it can remain as it has cracks in it. This is what happens when you choose your way -- a void remains in you. It blocks living water from flowing to you and causes you to live a parched, malnutritioned spiritual life. The living water represents God's assignments. When you reject an assignment from God, you reject His sustenance for the season that the assignment should have been fulfilled.

God will do everything that He can to help you accept His assignments for you. His assignments are life and blessing; rejecting them is death and curses. God sets His assignments in front of you as a display for you to choose. He doesn't dump any old thing for you to do. Every assignment He has for your life is well-thought- out and tailor- made for you. God wants you to win.

Deuteronomy 30:19-20 (NLT) - 19 "Today I have given you the choice between life and death, between blessings and curses. Now I call on heaven and earth to witness the choice you make. Oh, that you would choose life, so that you and your descendants might live!

20 You can make this choice by loving the Lord your God, obeying him, and committing yourself firmly to him. This is the key to your life. And if you love and obey the Lord, you will live long in the land the Lord swore to give your ancestors Abraham, Isaac, and Jacob."

In verse 20 we see that choosing life involves loving, obeying and committing yourself firmly to God. It also emphasizes that this is the key to your life. Obedience to God and His Word allows you to live long in the place that God has given you.

Believe What God Believes About You

Do you see the importance of believing God when He believes you can do what He's asking you to do? God asks you to do what He created you to do. He will only send you to places that will recognize your identity. The places He sends you have been prepared to receive you. He said in His Word that He will go before you and prepare the way. This is what God did for the Israelites.

Deuteronomy 1:33 (AMP) - 33 who went before you along the way, in fire by night and in a cloud by day, to seek a place for you to make camp and to show you the way in which you should go.

Deuteronomy 31:8 (NLT) - 8 Do not be afraid or discouraged, for the Lord will personally go ahead of you. He will be with you; he will neither fail you nor abandon you."

We see that God personally takes part in what He wants His people to do. You are God's "person" if you are part of His kingdom through Salvation. Therefore, you need to see yourself in light of these scriptures of God's personal attention, rather than the perspective of your past faults and failures.

The cure for faults and failures is repentance and a request for help from God. After God fixes these two problems in your life, you need to accept His solution by faith and look toward the mark that He's set before you. Paul speaks of pressing to reach the end of his race.

Philippians 3:14 (NLT) - 14 I press on to reach the end of the race and receive the heavenly prize for which God, through Christ Jesus, is calling us.

The goal you have for your life should be the same goal God has for your life. You should not wait for someone else to come alongside you. You should trust God and go alongside Him. God has a full detail of angelic protection for those who are found under the shadow of His wings. Psalm 91 paints a picture for us of how God protects those who seek shelter with Him.

Psalm 91:1& 11 (NLT) - 1 Those who live in the shelter of the Most High will find rest in the shadow of the Almighty.

11 For he will order his angels to protect you wherever you go.

Can you envision what this would look like in your life? A full detail of angels have been given charge over you. They have been ordered to protect you on every turn, keeping you from dashing your foot against an obstacle. God designed everything on this earth to support the people He sends to this earth. It is time for you to realize that God is for you and not against you.

Romans 8:31 (AMP) - 31 What then shall we say to all these things? If God is for us, who can be [successful] against us?

God has designed you to easily fulfill His plan. His grace on your life is sufficient to propel you to victory.

God's grace is available to you so that you can move forward with mighty power to do what God has designed you to do. Your decision to follow God's plan for your life is not without help and assistance from heaven. God is powerful and His support of us carries heavy weight in the heavenly realms and on the earth. As a matter of fact, Jesus gave us His own name to use as authority while dealing on earth.

Luke 9:1 (NLT) - 9 One day Jesus called together his twelve disciples and gave them power and authority to cast out all demons and to heal all diseases.

You have the authority to be here on earth and to work for the Kingdom of God and His plans. You have the right to take authority and to do what Jesus did on the earth, when He walked here. Jesus overcame everything the enemy has accused you of and paid the price on the cross for your redemption or debt to any sin. You have to receive what

Jesus has done and not reject His provision of love in order to benefit from His payment for you.

I believe that you are well able to do what God has designed you to do. I believe that what God wants you to do is not a mystery to you. Ask God to reveal it to you. He wants you to know and understand it. Don't agree with the enemy that you're not capable of doing what God shows you. Agree with God that He created you to fulfill it.

Go and take the land that God prepared for you when He formed heaven and earth. Don't hesitate or ask for permission, just accept God's assignment with joy.

Pray this now:

Father, I come before the Throne of Heaven and I accept your plans for me and reject with my own free will Satan's plan for my life. I willfully submit my gifts, abilities and identity to you Lord to be used for their intended purposes. Correct me in any area that I need to be recalibrated to your original design of me. I leave nothing for my enemies, but I receive all that you have planned for me to do and receive. I do not walk in deception anymore, instead I walk as a child of light. I confess that I am your child and you are my Father. I work for your Kingdom and your's alone. Not my will but Thine be done Father. Lord, I accept your identity reset. In Jesus' Name. Amen.

Scriptures

Exodus 23:22

2 Corinthians 4:2, 6

John 1:12

Psalm 139:23

FIONA PYSZKA

IDENTITY ANALYSIS

In this section you can take the opportunity to identify certain traits that you may have suppressed or have not understood. Take the time to answer the questions and then go to the end to understand what it means.

This is not a test to judge you, but one to help you understand that your God-given traits are important to God's purpose for you. Your design was specifically suited for your purpose.

Answer the following questions truthfully. Then analyze your answers with the information listed after the questions.

1. Do you like your height? _____ why or why not?

2. Do you like your skin color? _____ why or why not?

3. Do you like your ethnicity? _____ why or why not?

4. Do you like your birth order? _____ why or why not?

5. Do you like being loud or soft spoken? _____

6. Do you like to lead or follow? _____

Do people notice you in a crowded room, or do you seem invisible in a crowd? _____
How do you feel about being noticed or unnoticed?

7. Do you like your name? _____ why or why not?

8. Do you like the gender you were born with? __why or why not?

9. List the things about yourself that you like and do not like. Are there more things you like about yourself than don't like? Or is it vice versa?

What it all Means

For every part of yourself you do not like, ask God to show you why you may not like those things about you. There has to be a reason why they are negatives to you instead of a positive. When God created you this way, He planned a very successful and fulfilling destiny using these same traits. Repent if you see that it is because you wanted to be like someone you admire. Realize that the only person to admire in your design is God. Comparing yourself to someone else and then pointing out flaws about God's design of you is being ungrateful and unthankful for how He made you. These thoughts and feelings can hinder you from fulfilling the plan of God for your life.

Analyzing The Questions

There are some things about you that were given by man, those things could be changed by God if you desire them to be. Just like God changed Abram's name to Abraham He can do the same for you.

After you are finished analyzing your likes and dislikes, submit your list of who you are to God and let Him know that you are ready to follow His plan for your life. Allow Him to speak to you. Do what He says to do. Obedience is better than sacrifice.

Questions 1-3

Your height, skin color and ethnicity are all unchangeable things from God. These are necessary traits that God has put His favor on for you to be attractive to the assignment that He planned for you. Do not make light of these qualities, *embrace* them. Ask God to give you a love of these traits that He gave to you. Don't use them as an excuse for why you are not able to do what God asks you to do. Use them as a benefit, because that's what they were intended to be.

Question 4

Your birth order was perfectly planned by God because He knows all the days of your life. He knew them before any of them happened (see Psalms 139). We see Joseph, Jacob, Abel, and all of these people of the Bible have their birth order highlighted in some way. Don't complain about being the youngest, or oldest, or being stuck in the middle and feeling invisible all the time. Your spot in a family and time on the earth was perfectly planned.

Questions 5-6

Your natural ability to speak softly or have a voice that projects, no matter where you are, is a gift from God. Do not try to be what people would like you to be. Instead, develop your speech to be edifying to God. If your voice was designed to encourage, you're probably soft spoken. But, if your voice is loud, you're probably the one that speaks to storms as a regular routine. Don't misunderstand me, every believer can do what Jesus did. However, some assignments may require a louder voice or a softer voice. For example, John the Baptist most likely was a loud speaker. His message was repentance. He was making a way for Jesus.

If you are always called upon to lead even if you are not the designated leader, it means that God has designed you to be a leader. Your job is to develop the heart of God on leadership. Learn how to follow well before you step into leading. You can have a natural gift for leadership, but not use it effectively and people just "tolerate" you. However, if you learn to lead like God leads, then you will be miles ahead of your peers.

If you are always being recognized or called upon when you go anywhere, then you're designed to be noticed by people no matter where in the world you go. Embrace this and don't shy away from it. Present yourself honorably so that when people notice you, they notice God's character in you. The fruit of the Spirit should be a major focus of development in your life.

Question 7

Your name is a major part of your life. It is the label you tell people to put on you when thinking about you. That's right! You introduce yourself to the world using your name. If you don't like your name, no one else has a reason to like your name. You have to put value on your name so that people will respect it, love it and want to name their children that name. If for any reason your name reminds you of only negative experiences, change it. Ask God what you should change it to and do it. Don't delay! Do it right away. Make it an immediate project.

Question 8

Your gender is absolute! God did not give anyone in the history of mankind an option to change their gender. There is no record in the Bible of a God-sanctioned gender change. There are however, scriptures in Genesis that speak to a total destruction of the cities, Sodom and Gomorrah, whose people gave into unholy uses of their gender. God's choice of you being male or female was meticulously planned, just as He planned your purpose. Do not give into deception that lures you to call your gender a mistake, or a choice you can make. God made you absolutely male *or* female!

Question 9

If you find that you have more things that you dislike than like about yourself, you must take action now! It is critical to identify why you feel this way. To help you do this, take the list that you've created and pray over each item, asking God to reveal why you feel dislike instead of like for how He created you. Apply the principles in this book that will help you repair anything that may have marred your identity.

In Conclusion

This analysis is a way to identify how you feel about the traits that God created you with. If you have any issues with any part of who you are, I *urge* you to ask God to help you see the beauty in how He created you. Don't pray that God would change *how* He made you, ask Him to help *you* change to love your design.

You were beautifully and wonderfully made, a complete, one- of- a- kind masterpiece of the Creator of the universe.

Psalm 139:14 (NLT)14 Thank you for making me so wonderfully complex! Your workmanship is marvelous—how well I know it.

Other Books By The Author

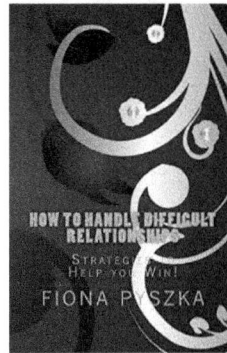

Visit fionainc.com for other personal development tools.

ABOUT THE AUTHOR

Fiona Pyszka is an international speaker, life coach, and author of 5 books, including her bestseller, *You Can Be Fearless*. She has an MBA in International Business from Regent University and is the president of Bless the Children Home Orphanage in Guyana.

Fiona's passion is to help people discover their purpose and walk in it. She's founded Fiona INC., a company that provides personal coaching development and tools for people of all ages and backgrounds.

An ordained minister, Fiona co-pastors with her husband Doug at Victory Christian Fellowship. She and Doug have been married for over 18 years, and they still reminisce about the amazing story of how God brought them together. They have two sons, Gabriel and Josiah, and live in central Pennsylvania.

www.ingramcontent.com/pod-product-compliance
Lightning Source LLC
Chambersburg PA
CBHW052008090426
42741CB00008B/1607